THE BATTLE FOR THE TRINITY

The Battle for the Trinity

The Debate over Inclusive God-Language

Donald G. Bloesch

Wipf and Stock Publishers
EUGENE, OREGON

Wipf and Stock Publishers
199 West 8th Avenue, Suite 3
Eugene, Oregon 97401

The Battle for the Trinity
The Debate over Inclusive God-Language
By Bloesch, Donald G.
©1985 Bloesch, Donald G.
ISBN: 1-57910-692-7
Publication date: July, 2001
Previously published by Vine Books, Servant Publications, 1985.

To my nephews,
David and Peter Bloesch

A new God is being formed in our hearts to teach us to level the heavens and exalt the earth and create a new world without masters and slaves, rulers and subjects.

—*Rosemary Ruether*

The doctrine of the Trinity remains in the twentieth century a test of Christian orthodoxy. Thus it is both desirable and essential that liturgical worship acknowledge God with the biblical names Father, Son, and Spirit.

—*Gail Ramshaw-Schmidt*

What is at stake here is the question of whether biblical statements about God—for example, about his Fatherhood in respect to Jesus Christ his incarnate Son—are related to what they claim to signify merely in a conventional way . . . or in a real way.

—*Thomas F. Torrance*

I cannot teach theology making use of inclusive language because I cannot participate in the promotion of false teachings, nor in the basis of all heresy—the denial of the authority of Scripture.

—*Leslie Zeigler*
(Bangor Theological Seminary)

Abbreviations for
Scriptural References

RSV - Revised Standard Version
KJV - King James Version
NKJV - New King James Version
NIV - New International Version

Contents

Foreword

DONALD BLOESCH HAS PAID feminist theologians the compliment, in this book, of taking them seriously. That is not at all a tribute to be scoffed at these days, for there are many theologians and biblical scholars in the church who pay little attention to such feminists, and that is a slight that may have serious consequences for the life of the church in the United States.

There have appeared, in the past ten years, numerous works by feminist theologians, which are not only reflections of developments taking place in the church but which have also had considerable influence on some of these developments. Feminism has affected the liturgy and worship of the church, its governing bodies, its witness, its doctrine, and its sacred literature. The women's movement can continue to be dismissed as a fad, only at the peril of the life of many members now in the church, and Donald Bloesch has realized that. He has read the feminist theological literature, and in this book, he critiques and challenges it. One can only hope that other equally dedicated theologians and biblical scholars will do the same.

There can be no doubt that several feminist theologians are in the process of laying the foundations for a new faith and a new church that are, at best, only loosely related to apostolic Christianity. Bloesch believes that feminist resymbolization of Christianity is leading to a new form of Gnosticism and of ancient Near Eastern goddess and fertility religion. I am sure that much of feminist theology is a return to Baalism. I am much less sure about its parallels with Gnosticism. But one thing is certain—many women, in their dedication to the feminist movement, are being slowly wooed into a new form of religion, widely at variance with the Christian faith. Most such women have no desire to desert their Christian roots, any more than many German Christians had when they accepted National Socialism's resymbolization of the faith in Nazi Germany (and Bloesch draws some interesting parallels between feminist theology and that movement). Nevertheless, the unwary and the unknowing are led astray, and the Body of Christ suffers for it.

In order to realize more fully what is happening, perhaps some theologians and biblical scholars need to imagine more realistically the depth of the hurt suffered by women in this country at the present time. The feminist movement has now gone far beyond its origins in the early suffrage movement, the civil rights movement of the sixties, and the initial impetus given to it by Betty Friedan's book, *The Feminine Mystique.* Modern American women now smart under not only unequal pay and inferior social status. They have come to sense that their struggle now has to do with their very being and purpose for being. Their hurt is no longer functional but ontological, no longer sociological but theological. And the result is that they are now acting and thinking ontologically and theologically. Feminism has invaded the realm of God, and in some instances, the God of the Christian faith has been replaced with a god or goddess of the feminists' making. The fathers have eaten sour grapes, and the daughters' teeth are set on edge. As a result, the feminist challenge is most assuredly the church's business.

Perhaps most distressing has been the church's reaction to that challenge. Certainly in bygone eras, the church fostered the subordination of women, and many of us still grieve over those Roman Catholic women denied ordination, those Southern Baptist women given seminary educations but denied a pulpit, those expert women preachers offered only assistants' roles. In guilty reaction to that, however, it does no good for ecclesiastical leaders heedlessly to encourage some women to alter the church's basic authority in the Scriptures. The freedom of both females and males rests firmly upon the foundation laid in Jesus Christ and mediated through the Scriptures. If that scriptural foundation is undermined, in the lectionary and prayers and instruction of the church, the gospel of freedom will be lost with it. It is not the Bible that is at fault, but the teaching of it.

In light of that, it is nothing short of astonishing that the whole educational wing of the church has neither admitted any responsibility for current feminist misinterpretations of the Bible nor mobilized any effort to correct those misinterpretations. On the contrary, many educators seem simply to accept feminists' positions without questioning the fundamental theological issues involved.

Dr. Bloesch does us the service in this book of raising those fundamental issues. Whether one agrees with all of his analysis or not, he points up the fact that we are indeed faced with a nationwide movement that is slowly but surely, through the efforts of its theologians, constructing a new church, on the basis of a new authority and theology. It is time that the church took a closer look at what is happening in it and to it.

—Elizabeth Achtemeier
Union Theological Seminary
Richmond, Virginia

Preface

WHEN SERVANT PUBLICATIONS asked me to expand a lecture
that I had presented to an interdenominational church renewal
conference in Chicago in March of 1984, it took me some time
to decide whether to give an affirmative reply. I had already
written a book on the problem of God-language and the
man-woman relationship (*Is the Bible Sexist?* Crossway Books,
1982). But many things have happened since then. The
problem in the churches has become far more acute: there are
now official committees at work revising the language about
God in prayer books and hymnals. The NCC *Inclusive
Language Lectionary* has been published and is being used in
many churches. In addition, the nature of religious language
has become a burning issue in contemporary theology. While I
agree that some old "generic" words are outmoded according
to contemporary usage, the attempt to deculturize often leads
to resymbolization in which the language of the church is set
in a new faith context.

It is my conviction that the current debate essentially
concerns the viability of the doctrine of the Trinity as well as
the authority of Scripture. We should be alert to the fact that
much deeper theological issues are involved than simply the
updating of language. In an age when the first person of the
Trinity is neuterized, the second person is spiritualized, and
the third person is sentimentalized (Michael Novak), the
church is challenged to retrieve the biblical and historical
meaning of the triune God, the living God of the Bible.

My purpose is not to give a systematic exposition of the
Trinity, but instead to show that the resymbolization of the
language of faith decisively alters the way in which God and

the world are conceived. I shall also endeavor to make clear that the debate on religious language has far-reaching implications for the understanding of the person and work of Jesus Christ.

This book should be seen not so much as a polemic against feminist theology (though it includes this), but as a warning against current attempts from various directions to alter the traditional language of faith. It is not only feminists but also process theologians, liberationists, existentialists, and neo-mystics who are pressing for drastic revisions in the formulation of faith. I shall try to show that meaning is integrally bound up in language and that when foundational symbols are altered, the meaning also changes. What we need is not a new mythical or symbolic framework for the faith but a fresh interpretation of the faith informed by the new light breaking forth from God's holy Word, a light that does not contradict but illumines what his inspired prophets and apostles said in the past.

Another issue dealt with in this book is the enigmatic relation between ideology and theology. Part of the problem today is that academic theology is becoming ever more vulnerable to ideological penetration, and this means that the message of faith is being adapted, often unwittingly, to the biases of the culture. It is not feminist theology per se, but cultural ideology (democratic egalitarianism, welfare liberalism, populism, ethnocentrism) that poses the principal threat to the faith of the church in Western culture at this time.

Theology needs to rediscover the early Barth and Kierkegaard if it is to resist the ideological allurements of our age. It was Barth appealing to the biblical principle of the infinite qualitative difference between time and eternity (rediscovered by Kierkegaard) who warned against the cultural synthesis perpetrated by the Neo-Protestants and their descendants the German Christians, those who tried to bring the faith into alignment with the ideology of National Socialism. Despite the fact that his political sympathies were on the side of the left, Barth was compelled to break with his religious socialist friends on this very issue—the transcendence of the claims of faith over the demands of ideology.

I write as an evangelical Christian who shares the concerns of those in the women's liberation movement for fair practice in employment and wage benefits. I also believe that there is a biblical basis for women in leadership positions—both civil and spiritual. My book *Is the Bible Sexist?* was greeted with a signal lack of enthusiasm by both the ideological left and right for its effort to break through the present-day impasse separating Christian feminists and patriarchalists or traditionalists. At the same time, it was applauded by many Christians, both men and women, whose loyalty to the gospel supersedes ideological commitments.

Though I regard myself as pro-woman, I sense in the modern feminist movement an ominous drift toward goddess spirituality, which calls people into a new faith orientation. Many women in the teaching ministry of the church, such as Elizabeth Achtemeier, Leslie Zeigler, and Elisabeth Elliot, have similar misgivings. The reappearance of the heresy of Gnosticism is especially evident in the cult of the goddess. Just as the ancient Gnostics sought a God above and behind the triune God of historical Christian faith, so their descendants are trying to do much the same thing.

Despite these profound reservations, I do not wish to leave the impression that my reaction to feminist theology is totally negative. We can learn from this new adversary to traditional Christian faith, just as we can learn from both process and liberation theologies. Feminist theology, for example, has given us an expanded notion of sin. In addition to viewing sin as unbelief and pride, we also need to see that it entails oppression and exploitation as well as a disturbing acquiescence to these social evils. This theology reminds us, moreover, that Christ is model as well as Savior. Our Lord's treatment of women as well as of cultural minorities can be a salutary example for our time. The interdependence of man and woman, as advocated by biblically qualified feminists,* is a welcome alternative to both the servile dependence of woman on man (as found in patriarchy) and the independence of woman from man (as found in mainstream and radical feminism).

Where feminist theology makes its most signal contribution to theology is the way in which it calls us to reexamine the language of faith. It reminds us that much of the language of Scripture is symbolic and pictorial, that it points beyond itself to realities that cannot be directly apprehended by theoretical reason. If we think of God as Father in a univocal way, then God becomes male, and this is indeed idolatry.

The question nonetheless persists: Do the foundational symbols of the faith impart real knowledge, or do they merely evoke feelings of reverence and delight toward a God who is basically ineffable and undefinable, who will always remain hidden from human sight and understanding?

This book is primarily a discussion of theological epistemology with special bearing on the doctrines of the Trinity and the incarnation. It is therefore relevant for all Christians who seek a firmer foundation for their faith than that presently offered by a great many self-styled theological experts who believe that the main barrier to faith lies in the archaic language in which the faith has come to us rather than in the scandal of the cross, the gospel of the vicarious, atoning sacrifice of Christ for the sins of a fallen human race.

---

*Since this position is not characteristic of those who identify themselves as feminists, it might be better termed a "covenantalist" approach. A covenantalist affirms that the two sexes are created for fellowship with God and with one another. When we remain true to the divine imperative, we shall inherit the divine promises. See my *Is the Bible Sexist?*, pp. 84ff.

Acknowledgments

I wish to acknowledge the solid help I have received from my wife Brenda in the areas of research and copyediting. I am also indebted to the following persons for their assistance in preparing this manuscript for publication: Professor Harold Nebelsick of Louisville Presbyterian Theological Seminary; Professors Ralph Quere and Frank Benz of Wartburg Theological Seminary; Professor Douglas Meeks of Eden Theological Seminary; Rev. Gerald Sanders of the Biblical Witness Fellowship in the United Church of Christ; Dr. Frederick Trost, Conference Minister of the United Church of Christ in Wisconsin; Diana Leonard, reference librarian at the University of Dubuque Theological Seminary; and Ralph Carr, my student assistant. My secretary at the seminary, Peg Saunders, has typed this manuscript with her usual diligence and care. I also gratefully acknowledge the permission of the Abingdon Press to include the lengthy quotation from Samuel Laeuchli's book *The Language of Faith* (1962), on p. 49.

ONE

The Current Debate

A Growing Controversy

Two decades ago the principal issues in the church were whether the Bible should be demythologized (Bultmann) or deliteralized (Tillich). Now the main issue is whether the Bible should be resymbolized. Various theological movements in the church today are pressing for the resymbolization of the Christian faith, but none is so powerful and vocal as feminist theology. What is needed, the feminists say, is a new imagery that will reflect the holistic vision of modern culture. The biblical metaphors drawn from a patriarchal and hierarchical culture are considered dualistic and monarchial and should be replaced by images more in tune with the spirit of the times.

Patriarchalists, those who see the man as head of the woman and the voice of authority in the family, not surprisingly resist such efforts, fearing that any change in the language of faith that would call into question the sovereignty of God and the lordship and headship of Jesus Christ over his church would threaten family solidarity and social structure.[1] Opposition to proposed changes in language in liturgy and worship also comes from traditionalists who simply have a romantic nostalgia for the past.

There are others within the church, however, who are equally disturbed by the feminist demands for resymbolizing the language of faith. Their concern is that the very meaning of

1

the faith might be changed, that the particularistic claims of
the Bible might be compromised. These are people who may
well be sympathetic to the demands of women for equality of
opportunity and who may well be open to women in positions
of leadership in the church. Yet they are alarmed at what a shift
in metaphors will do to such doctrines as the Trinity and the
incarnation. I align myself with this group, though this does
not mean that I am unwilling to listen to what feminists are
saying in this crucial area.

Besides feminism, other theological movements seeking to
alter the basic symbolism of the faith include process theology,
liberation theology, and neomysticism. I shall be saying more
on this subject in chapter four, but for our purposes here it is
well to recognize that such movements reflect a growing
discontent in the academic circles of the church with the
traditional language of faith, which no longer seems to speak
to people of culture. As avant-garde theologians see it, such
language is not able to connect with modernity, and this
means that the Christian faith can then no longer penetrate the
enclaves of the culture.

The conflict on this issue is accelerating as policy-making
boards and agencies of the church become more receptive to
feminist demands. There are currently committees at work in
nearly all the mainline Protestant denominations revising the
language of liturgy and compiling new hymnals. A United
Church of Christ document says that we should "avoid use of
masculine-biased language applied to the Trinity as in 'Father,
Son, and Holy Ghost.'"[2] We are also instructed to avoid the
use of masculine pronouns and adjectives in reference to God,
such as *he* or *his*. We are even asked to abandon masculine role
names for God including "Lord," "King," "Father," "Master,"
and "Son." At the United Methodist General Conference in
Baltimore in May of 1984, Methodists were urged to begin
finding new ways of referring to deity, such as alternating male
and female pronouns or using genderless terms.[3] The majority
of an eleven-member committee in the Church of Scotland

recommends a "restrained and sensitive use of feminine language both to describe and to address God."[4] The new *Inclusive Language Lectionary* put out by the National Council of Churches in October of 1983 has heightened the controversy by deleting references to Christ as "Lord" and "Son" and by calling God "Father and Mother."

The not-surprising openness of many feminists (even some evangelical feminists) to goddess spirituality augments the growing polarization in the church today. At a conference sponsored by the C.J. Jung Center at the Montview Boulevard Presbyterian Church in Denver in April of 1984, feminist author Jean Bolen encouraged her hearers to offer prayers to such goddesses as Athena, Demeter, Artemis, and Aphrodite.[5] While discounting these as literal or anthropomorphic deities, she nonetheless accepts them as powerful symbols of creative powers within all of us.

Not only conservatives, but also those who might be described as moderate or mainstream in theological orientation are beginning to react against this concerted attempt to alter liturgy and spirituality. Elizabeth Achtemeier, Old Testament scholar and teacher at Union Theological Seminary in Richmond, Virginia, has this to say about the NCC Lectionary:

> In short, the canon of the Christian faith has been turned into a propaganda document for a special-interest group. Faith has become subservient to ideology, scholarly honesty to current notions. The authority operative here is no longer the canon, but the views of radical women's groups.[6]

John Meyendorff, professor of church history at St. Vladimir's Orthodox Seminary in Crestwood, N.Y., gives this dour appraisal: "Any translation is always an interpretation, but this translation departs from the intention of the writers. It's a deception. . . . It shows a deplorable attitude and will bring in more dissension between the churches."[7] Bruce Metzger of

Princeton Theological Seminary, who chairs the committee on reworking the Revised Standard Version of the Bible, is equally forthright: "The changes introduced in language relating to the Deity are tantamount to rewriting the Bible. As a Christian, and as a scholar, I find this altogether unacceptable. It will divide the church, rather than work for ecumenical understanding."[8]

Not all feminists go along with the demands for resymbolization. While open to supplemental language in which feminine images for God are sometimes used in prayer and worship, Gail Ramshaw-Schmidt trenchantly perceives that language revision could call into question such crucial doctrines as the Trinity. "The doctrine of the Trinity," she says, "remains in the twentieth century a test of Christian orthodoxy. Thus it is both desirable and essential that liturgical worship acknowledge God with the biblical names Father, Son, and Spirit."[9] With curious inconsistency, however, she insists that masculine pronouns for God create an unnecessary offense to women and ought to be avoided wherever possible.

Types of Feminism

Because feminism is not a monolithic movement, we need to differentiate between its various strands. First of all, there are the more conservative feminists who while committed to challenging patriarchal subordinationism are not willing to abandon the historic language of the faith. They may well press for making people language more inclusive, replacing such terms as "man," "men," and "mankind" by "people," "humans," and "humankind," or something comparable. Yet they balk at any basic revision of the language about God, since this indicates for them a change in faith orientation. Among such persons are Martha Stortz, Paul Jewett, Thomas Finger, Jean Caffey Lyles, Patricia Gundry, and to a lesser extent Gail Ramshaw-Schmidt, though a few of these are willing to appropriate feminine imagery for God wherever feasible.

Then there are the reformist feminists who seek a wholesale revision of God-language in order to counter alleged sexism in this language and to prepare the way for a more inclusive family of God. They do not wish to deny the Trinity, but they urge more inclusive language for the Trinity such as Creator, Redeemer, and Sanctifier. God becomes "Eternal Spirit" or "the Holy One" rather than "Heavenly Father." Christ is described as "Child" rather than "Son, as "Friend" rather than "Lord" and "Master." Often the Holy Spirit is referred to as "she." These feminists wish to work within the church as a reforming element, committed to the goal of a purified Christianity, purged of sexism and patriarchalism. Many (though not all) of these people are attracted to the ancient myth of androgyny in which God is portrayed as female as well as male. Leading thinkers in this group include Rosemary Ruether, Sallie McFague, Dorothee Soelle, Anne Carr, Patricia Wilson-Kastner, Susan Thistlethwaite, Joan Chamberlain Engelsman, Virginia Ramey Mollenkott, Elisabeth Schüssler-Fiorenza, Nancy Hardesty, and Letty Russell.

Finally there are the revolutionary or radical feminists who regard Christianity as incurably patriarchal and sexist and who therefore opt for a new religion, one that proves to be a form of nature mysticism. Mary Daly began as a reformer in the church, but she has since thrown her Christian commitment overboard and embarked on a quest for a spirituality based exclusively on woman's consciousness. Naomi Goldenberg calls for the restoration of the religion of witchcraft, which is more in tune with the cycles of nature. Other women who are attracted to a naturistic mysticism are Meinrad Craighead, Starhawk (Miriam Simos), Sheila D. Collins, Charlene Spretnak, Carol Ochs, Rita Gross, Carol Christ, Judith Plaskow, Shirley Ann Ranck, and Penelope Washbourn.

We should also note those women in the church who find themselves at odds with ideological feminism but nonetheless support the movement for women's rights within society.

Some would be opposed to women's ordination, but others would be very supportive of women in positions of spiritual leadership in the church. Among such persons are Elizabeth Achtemeier, Jeanne Kun, Ronda Chervin, Leslie Zeigler, Sister Miriam Murphy, Lucetta Mowry, Susan Foh, Marion Battles, and Juli Loesch.[10]

We should keep in mind that ideological feminism includes not only women but also men who seek to break down hierarchical structures in church and society and who are committed to the cultural vision of a holistic humanity. Among male theologians and other scholars who espouse the cause of feminism in varying degrees are Burton H. Throckmorton, Jr., Matthew Fox, Paul Jewett, Donald Gelpi, Thomas D. Parker, Robin Scroggs, Tom Driver, Leonard Swidler, Fritjof Capra, John Cobb, Charles Hartshorne, Mark Branson, Harold Oliver, and Jürgen Moltmann.

Theologians and Philosophers behind Feminism

Moltmann's position in particular is seen as lending support to the feminist life- and world-view. Moltmann conceives of God as bisexual and regards the Spirit and the *Shekinah* as denoting the feminine principle within the Godhead. In place of monotheism, which supposedly is tied to patriarchy, and pantheism, which is associated with matriarchy, he proposes "panentheism," which is rooted in androgyny. In panentheism God and the world are not identical but interdependent.

Drawing upon Hegelian insights, Moltmann speaks of a history within God whereby God unfolds himself in the world of time and space. No longer a sovereign being transcendent over the world, God now becomes "the event of self-liberating love" or the eternally "self-communicating love." The Trinity is no longer a supernatural fellowship beyond history, but an eschatological process within history in which we can be included. He rejects the traditional Christian doctrine of the creation of the world out of nothing (*creatio ex nihilo*) and instead interprets creation in terms of emanation in the sense of a divine overflowing. In his view "all people and things . . . partake of the 'inner-trinitarian life' of God."[11] The unity of the Trinity is to be found in suffering love. Moltmann acknowledges his affinities to the process philosophy of Whitehead as well as to the dynamic idealism of Hegel. We see in him the convergence of process theology, liberation theology, and feminist theology.

Another theologian heavily influenced by Hegel and in whom the Neoplatonic influence is equally conspicuous is Paul Tillich. Tillich, too, has proved to be a significant source of support for Christian feminists. Like Meister Eckhart and other mystics in the Neoplatonic tradition, Tillich speaks of a God above God, the infinite ground and depth of all being. At the same time, Tillich aligns himself with the innerworldly mysticism of Boehme and the later Schelling in which this infinite ground becomes a source of creativity and power at work within the world. We make contact with God not by ascending above nature, but in descending into the depths of nature.[12] This is why he calls God both the infinite abyss and the eternal ground. We perceive God not in a world beyond nature, but precisely in the rhythm and rhapsody of nature and also in its incongruities and discords. God is the infinite in the finite, the spiritual in the material. No wonder Tillich calls his position an "ecstatic naturalism."

Tillich sees God as essentially Spirit or Spiritual Presence, and Spirit, it seems, is conceived basically as feminine rather than masculine. He describes the action of the Spirit as "the mother-quality of giving birth, carrying, and embracing, and, at the same time, of calling back, resisting independence of the created, and swallowing it."[13] God is pictured as "the divine life . . . actualizing itself in inexhaustible abundance," rather than the divine act that calls the worlds into being.[14] At the same time, Tillich insists that the true God—the infinite depth of all being—transcends the polarity between subject and object, masculine and feminine, and is best understood as suprapersonal rather than personal per se.

In the process theology of Charles Hartshorne, who gladly acknowledges his commitment to feminism, God is conceived of as bisexual with the feminine aspect being dominant. That is to say, God is understood primarily as the receptacle of the world's impressions rather than as a creative agent acting on the world. God is the Cosmic Consciousness inclusive of all that is good and beautiful in the world rather than an almighty Creator and Redeemer. Hartshorne contends that the picture of God "as all-creative, all-determining Cause, effect of, influenced by, nothing" can no longer be seriously entertained.[15] "Much more appropriate is the idea of a mother, influencing, but sympathetic to and hence influenced by, her child and delighting in its growing creativity and freedom."[16] Thus God is much more the sympathy that soothes than the fire that burns. Hartshorne has no compunction in referring to God as "He-She," signifying that God is both creative and receptive. Indeed, he refers to God as "the supreme Creative and Receptive Spirit of the cosmos."[17] A growing number of feminist theologians draw generously from the tradition of both process philosophy and theology, whether this be the Hartshornian, Whiteheadian, Teilhardian, or Hegelian brands.[18]

Other philosophers who have a special appeal to feminists include Carl Jung (who resurrected the myth of androgyny), Wilhelm Reich, William Blake, Jacob Boehme, Herbert Marcuse, Simone de Beauvoir, Theodore Roszak, William James, Alfred North Whitehead, Teilhard de Chardin, and to a lesser degree Plato, Aristotle, Plotinus, and Valentinus. Feminist theology seems particularly open to neomysticism as we see this in Schelling, Tillich, Schleiermacher, Kazantzakis, and Teilhard de Chardin (who envisioned an androgynous mystical unification as the climax of history). In this kind of mysticism we find God not by trying to escape from the world or transcend the world but by immersing ourselves more deeply in it. God is experienced in the depths rather than the heights, in the instincts and sensations rather than in the world of pure spirit

The Gnostic Connection

The surprising affinity between modern feminism and Gnosticism also needs to be explored.[19] In the tradition of Gnosticism, eternity is found by looking inwards; the universal awareness of divinity residing in humanity takes precedence over the particularity of a divine revelation in history, and self-understanding (*gnosis*) is regarded as superior to simple faith in a living God. "For the gnostics, " says one renowned scholar, "bisexuality is an expression of perfection; it is only the earthly creation which leads to a separation of the original divine unity, which holds for the whole Pleroma."[20] In Christian tradition it was the Gnostics who spoke of God as both Father and Mother and conceived of God as bisexual— the feminine element being the Eternal Silence and the masculine the Primal Depth (*Bythos*). In Gnostic speculation the feminine dimension of the sacred was also represented by the Holy Spirit and Wisdom (*Sophia*) and the masculine by the Demiurge, an inferior deity, the creator of our particular world; the last was often equated with Jehovah, the God of Israel. Though Gnosticism occasionally made use of trinitarian terminology, basically it saw God not as a Trinity, but as a dyad whose nature includes both masculine and feminine elements.[21]

Feminist spirituality has many things in common with Gnosticism, though it also contains thrusts that point in another direction.[22] (This is why it is more appropriate to view it as a form of Neo-Gnosticism). The conception of a primal unity encompassing both masculine and feminine and needing to be recovered or rediscovered is prominent in feminism (as in Gnosticism). A turning away from procreation and motherhood in order to pursue life's goal is characteristic of both movements. While the Gnostics envisioned the return of spirit to its divine source and ground, the feminists look forward to a holistic humanity—the complement of a bisexual divinity.

The ancient prison motif, prominent in Gnosticism, reappears in feminism. In Gnosticism, spirit is believed to be encased in materiality and temporality and needs to be released in order to be reunited with the kingdom of light. In feminism it is commonly held that both men and women are caught in a web of alienation and fear, engendered by a patriarchal culture, and need to be set free in order to realize their full potential as human beings liberated from sexual stereotyping. The Gnostics sought to facilitate the awakening of the "seed of light" residing in humanity. Similarly, feminists see their mission as the awakening of the consciousness of living in a male-female world (rather than a world that is exclusively male-oriented).

While for some of the Gnostics "perfect knowledge" is manifested in "fearlessness and independence,"[23] so feminists regard the quest for autonomy as the indication of an enlightened consciousness. Many of the radical feminists celebrate nature and even uphold a polymorphous sexuality. But this, too, is anticipated in Gnosticism: the libertines among the Gnostics exaulted in a vitalistic intoxication of the senses, viewing it as a freedom from the taboos and restrictions that characterize the beginners in the religious life.

A Gnostic thrust can be detected not only in feminist theology but also in the writings of such neomystics as Heidegger, Jung,[24] Tillich, and MacGregor.[25] It was the Gnostics who misunderstood and sought to subvert the Christian doctrine of the Trinity. The Gnostics as well as the Neoplatonic mystics conceived of a God above God, the "Eternal Silence" or "Void" beyond the Trinity.

Where the Issue Lies

The debate in the church today is not primarily over women's rights but over the doctrine of God. Do we affirm a God who coexists as a fellowship within himself, that is, who is trinitarian, or a God who is the impersonal or suprapersonal ground and source of all existence? Do we believe in a God who acts in history, or in a God who simply resides within nature? Are we committed to a God who saves the world by a sacrificial act of undeserved compassion, or a God who moves the world by the lure of his magnetic love (the God of process theology)? Do we believe in a God who created the world out of nothing or in a God whose infinite fecundity gave rise to a world that is inseparable from his own being? Do we affirm a God of the heights or a God of the depths?

Also of crucial significance in this debate is the adequacy of human language in describing God. Are the words of faith only ciphers of transcendence (Jaspers, Buri), only symbols that point to an ineffable ground of all being, or can such words give us real knowledge of the eternal God? Did God really reveal himself decisively and definitively (though not exhaustively) in the person of his Son Jesus Christ, a man who lived and died in history, or is Jesus Christ only a symbol of divine-human unity, or of transformed human identity, a possibility within the reach of all of us? Is the language of faith the indispensable means for knowing God, or does it stand in the way of knowledge of God?

The conflict as I see it is really between the historic Christian faith and a refurbished form of the old heresy of Gnosticism. It reflects the historical imcompatibility between biblical theism and Gnostic and Neoplatonic mysticism. It is already antic-ipated in the Old Testament in the rival claims of the monotheistic religion of the prophets and the naturistic religion of the fertility cults. What is at stake is not simply the doctrine of the Trinity but the integrity and identity of the church of Jesus Christ. It seems that we have to choose between the latest form of culture-religion and the prophetic religion of the biblical and catholic heritage of the church.

This controversy is therefore much more serious than most people who prefer to stand on the sidelines are willing to acknowledge. There can be no neutrality where the faith of the church is called into question. Feminist theology is only the tip of the iceberg. It is only one manifestation of the resurgence of the pre-Christian gods of ancient mythology, the gods of the barbarian tribes, as they seek to make a comeback in a time when our culture languishes in a metaphysical vacuum.

TWO

The Enigma of God-Language

Religious Language and the Knowledge of God

The crucial question concerning God-language is whether such language gives a true knowledge or merely a symbolic awareness of the ultimate reality we call God. This is a debate that goes back to the earliest centuries of the church. The Gnostics maintained that God, who stands over against and behind the fallen world of materiality, is ineffable and impassible but that we can make contact with divinity by methodical introspection and ritual purification. The tradition of Neoplatonic mysticism, which has infiltrated both Roman Catholicism and Eastern Orthodoxy, envisioned a God beyond temporal distinctions, even beyond reason. God was portrayed as imageless transcendence, and the goal was to get beyond words into the eternal silence. It was said that we can only speak of what God is not (the way of negation), that all positive affirmations of God are inadequate.

The church fathers and medieval theologians generally sought to combat skepticism about knowing and speaking of God. Even though they acknowledged that God is nameless in the sense that our words cannot adequately express his essence, they insisted that he can be named on the basis of the likeness that can be discerned in the relationship between God and his creatures, a relationship that is most clearly apprehended in faith. Yet it was also said that God is more unlike than like humankind, that God cannot be grasped by human conception or encompassed by human imagination. The legacy of Neoplatonic mysticism in Catholic theology had far-reaching implications for spirituality, for it was contended that the highest prayer is beyond words and concepts and that the historical Jesus is only a sacramental sign that enables us to ascend to the eternal God, who is outside of temporality and materiality.

Thomas Aquinas made some important distinctions in language usage that have left a lasting imprint on both philosophy and theology.[1] To speak univocally of something means to speak literally: our words fully convey what they are intended to signify. There is an exact correspondence between the sign and what it signifies. Because God is not homogeneous with man, we can never speak univocally of God. To speak equivocally is to use words that carry quite different meanings when applied to both God and the creature. Metaphorical words are dissimilar to what is described, and while there may be a suggested likeness between the sign and what it signifies, there is no conceptual knowledge. A metaphor is an anomalous rather than a precise description of reality.

At best, Thomas suggested, we can speak of God only analogically, in which there is a partial resemblance between our words and the transcendent reality to which they point. The resemblance is based on proportionality rather than identity. While analogy yields real knowledge, it is not complete knowledge.[2] Analogy, moreover, does not overcome the infinite distance between God and man, for, Thomas insisted, God is always more unlike than like the creaturely world that reflects his glory. Although we begin from below in our analogizing, the norm for the truth of our analogy lies in the object, i.e., in God's self-revelation, rather than in the subject.

The Enlightenment philosopher Immanuel Kant denied that we can ever have conceptual or theoretical knowledge of the thing in itself (*Ding an sich*), the noumenal that stands behind the phenomenal or the world of appearance. Yet he allowed for the fact that we can have a symbolic knowledge of God, which is not objective knowledge, but intuitive awareness. Since Kant, a major strand in theology has taken pains to distinguish between the objective knowledge that pertains only to the empirical world and symbolic awareness that gives us a deeper understanding of self but not a life- and world-view.

Not all theology, of course, accepts this bifurcation. Neo-naturalism (Wieman, Macintosh) holds that we can have objective knowledge of God via our senses because God is an objective reality in nature and history. Conservative evangelicals like Gordon Clark, Carl Henry, and Ronald Nash, maintain that we have univocal, and not merely analogical, knowledge of God because God has given us a verbal revelation of himself—accessible to reason and the senses.

Most modern theology, however, is closer to Tillich and the existentialists who are skeptical concerning the possibility of attaining conceptual or propositional knowledge of God. What revelation gives us, said Tillich, is not objective knowledge, but a true awareness. It was his position that we could speak about God symbolically, but this must not be taken to mean simply poetically or intuitively. A symbol, unlike a sign, participates in the reality to which it points. In the first volume of his *Systematic Theology* Tillich maintains that the one literal statement we can make of God is that he is Being-itself (*ipsum esse*). Yet in his second volume Tillich contends that all language about God partakes of the symbolic and that the knowledge of God is more a quest than a possession.[3]

Paul Ricoeur, whose affinities are with existentialist theology and philosophy, holds that the primary language of faith is metaphorical and the secondary language conceptual.[4] The sacred is first intuited by means of religious experience and then rationally explained. When translating from the meta-phorical into the conceptual, we must make sure that the second is continually funded by the first, or the result will be a new religion. Even conceptual discourse cannot be wholly divested of its symbolic roots, or else it provides not a bridge but a barrier between the original experience and rational interpretation. The goal of interpretation, he maintains, is to return to the experience that the primary language expresses. In the case of Christianity, this experience is the parabolic redescription of reality in terms of the new reality of the kingdom of God.

In my judgment, the most penetrating and provocative book on this subject in recent years is that by the feminist theologian Sallie McFague—*Metaphorical Theology*.[5] McFague distin-guishes between metaphor and symbol: a metaphor "finds the vein of similarity in the midst of dissimilars," whereas a symbol "rests on similarity already present and assumed."[6] She here closely associates symbol with analogy, which indicates a partial correspondence between the sign and what it signifies. A metaphor gives not exact knowledge (as in univocity) or even proportional knowledge (as in analogy) but seminal insight. She endorses Dillistone's view that while analogy tends toward petrification, metaphor moves toward renova-tion.[7] A metaphor redescribes reality in terms of a bold, imaginative vision rather than simply portraying reality as that which is already given. Whereas symbol and analogy assume "an order and unity already present waiting to be realized," metaphor "projects, tentatively, a possible transformed order and unity yet to be realized."[8]

McFague goes along with Paul Ricoeur and David Tracy that every religion is based on a root metaphor, a pictorial description of reality which governs reflection upon that reality. For her, the root metaphor of Christianity is the kingdom of God understood as the religio-cultural movement for human liberation. The model of "Father" only connotes that God acts in a fatherly way, but this leaves us room, on the basis of the biblical testimony as well as religious experience, to affirm that God also acts in a "motherly way." We are therefore free to call God Mother as well as Father and to refer to God as "she" as well as "he." This must not be taken to mean that God is a person but that personal metaphors can enable us to relate to ultimate reality, the creative source and ground of being, which is also called the New Being or the unconditioned.

I agree with some of the participants in this discussion that religious language is originally symbolic and that when the reality to which it points is interpreted in the light of religious tradition and experience it necessarily becomes conceptual. A concept is an abstract term that roughly corresponds to what it purports to signify; a symbol is a pictorial term that brokenly reflects what it is intended to signify. Whereas the meaning of a concept can be rationally determined, the meaning of a symbol can only be intuitively grasped. A myth is a symbol in narrative form. Torrance persuasively argues that in theology we proceed from *mythos* to *logos*, "from thinking projectively in pictures and images to thinking in terms of structured imageless relations."[9] Yet we must not jettison the symbolism of faith in our theologizing but instead seek always to interpret it. The symbol still continues to have a normative authority to which conceptual thinking is subordinate. At the same time, conceptual thinking enables us to determine which symbols are really germane to the faith and which are inauthentic or peripheral.

McFague is not far from the truth when she argues that theological language "is certainly a mix of metaphorical and conceptual language."[10] Yet she fails to perceive that symbol or analogy is more basic to the language of revelation than metaphor. In her theology, it seems that the language of faith verges on equivocity rather than analogy.

The Munich theologian Wolfhart Pannenberg is quite firm that the language of faith is the language of doxology, which is closer to metaphor than to analogy in the Thomistic sense.

Analogy is not midway between univocity and equivocity, but is really a form of the latter.[11] "In the very act of adoration," he says, "our words, since they are transferred to God, become equivocal in relationship to their ordinary meaning, no matter how well founded and free from arbitrary derivation this use of words may be."[12] Acknowledging the influence of Immanuel Kant, Pannenberg says "the analogy exists only in the language, not between the language and God himself."[13] Against Barth he affirms that all analogizing proceeds from below to above, and "it is precisely this point that is the root of the inadequacy of all human knowledge of God."[14] Because Pannenberg sees the resurrection of Jesus as proleptic of the world transformation at the consummation of history, when we shall know even as we are known, the biblical revelation gives only a faint intimation of God, who is still very much veiled to historical understanding. It cannot give us the precision we need to speak of God with any assurance that our words have a real correspondence to reality.

In his view,

> The correspondence of our words to God himself has not already been decided, but is yet to be decided. This temporal difference between our speech about God and its fulfillment by God himself cannot be expressed by means of the concept of analogy. Judged from our standpoint, the concepts by which we praise God's essence become equivocal in the act of the sacrifice of praise. At the same time, however, we utter them in the hope of a fulfillment which by far overcomes the distance fixed in the analogy.[15]

Pannenberg acknowledges that we can speak more precisely about the acts of God in history than about God himself. This is to speak of God indirectly, not directly. Yet even our kerygmatic speech about a specific divine act "already presupposes a doxological element, viz., that God is an acting person."[16] Since only the eschaton will disclose what really happened when Jesus Christ rose from the dead, we can now speak of this event only in symbolic form. I here agree with Kenneth Hamilton's stricture on this kind of speculation:

> Hence Pannenberg has emptied the resurrection of all actuality, and has slipped back into a mythic form of interpreting the person of Jesus Christ. The incarnate Word is forbidden to speak to us really, and it is forced to give no more than symbolic utterance. Revelation is put into the future. The Father may yet speak—but He has not already spoken decisively in the Son.[17]

Avery Dulles distinguishes between symbols and analogies in his relevant and brilliant study, *Models of Revelation.*[18] While analogies are self-interpreting, symbols may require further explanation. Dulles defines a symbol as "a sign pregnant with a plenitude of meaning which is evoked rather than explicitly stated."[19] Symbols do not simply point to a supratemporal reality but lead into this reality. What the symbols of revelation give us is "participatory awareness." This awareness is not divorced from thought, however, but gives rise to thought and shapes thought. While not denying a propositional dimension to revelation, Dulles basically understands revelation as "symbolic-evocative communication." He holds that symbols have cognitive value, and some symbols are unalterable. Faith is not a steady and certain knowledge of the divine promises given to us in Scripture (Calvin) but "a stretching forth of the mind toward an insight not yet given, or not clearly given."[20]

While concurring with Dulles that symbols have a cognitive content and that they refer to objective realities and not simply to an ineffable presence of the divine in all things, I believe that he is still too close to the Tillichian and existentialist understanding of symbols as yielding an awareness of an indefinable reality rather than knowledge of a definitive revelation of God in history. For Dulles, revelation gives clues too deep for words, and therefore symbols are necessary to "bridge contrasts that defy conceptual integration."[21]

Dulles calls his position "symbolic realism," meaning that the symbols of faith have an objective reference and are not to be understood as projections of the imagination upon the screen of history (as in Bultmann). Yet the question remains whether he is able to maintain the objective and historical character of revelation as something given once for all in the salvific events recorded in the Bible. When he denies that revelation has any formal existence apart from faith and when he affirms that revelation is an immanent rather than external ground for the life of the church, we can see how far he is from evangelical understanding. It seems that for him revelation is an ongoing process in the life of the church in which the church plumbs "the depths of its own self-consciousness,"[22] rather than a Word from the beyond that stands in judgment over the church and over the believer. The task of theology, he says, is to "retrieve the wealth of meaning and wisdom contained in the multiple sources"[23] of church tradition rather than submit to a definitive revelation given in the Bible which is conveyed through symbolic language to be sure, but nonetheless contains definite promises and imperatives that can be directly applied to the life of the church and the world.

Symbols and Revelation

It is obvious by now that the term "symbol" is used today in many different senses, and this is why theologians are often talking past one another rather than really coming to grips with the issues that divide them. I contend that symbol must be taken to denote any kind of imagistic language whose meaning cannot be directly comprehended by theoretical reason. A symbol points beyond itself to a reality that can only be dimly perceived by the senses or faintly understood by reason. A symbol is a graphic image that brokenly reflects what it purports to describe.

Symbols may be either metaphors or analogies, and these are not the same. I agree with Thomas and Barth that analogical knowledge is real knowledge, whereas metaphorical knowledge is only intuitive awareness or tacit knowledge. An analogy conveys conceptual content; a metaphor alludes to that which escapes conceptualization.[24] To say that God is a Rock or Fortress is metaphorical, but to call God Father or Lord is analogical. A metaphor connotes a suggested likeness between two things that are manifestly dissimilar, whereas an analogy presupposes an underlying similarity or congruity in the midst of real difference. The language of faith contains metaphor, analogy, and concept, but what is conveyed is something much more than mystical insight or self-understanding. Faith language communicates by the power of the Spirit a real, objective disclosure of the living God in actual human history, a disclosure which can be only partially grasped by reason, but which does not entirely elude reason. While rationalism reduces mystery to meaning that is clear and distinct and mysticism dissolves meaning into mystery, biblical religion affirms that meaning shines through mystery.

Theologians do not wish to talk about God in exclusively empirical terms, for this would be anthropomorphic univocation. Nor should they be forced to speak of him in nonempirical terms, the way of metaphysical equivocation. Instead, they may speak of him in symbolic or imagistic terms, the way of analogy. Even when they employ concepts in their language about God (as they must), these concepts are never univocal but still continue to partake of the analogical or symbolic. Our conceptual language about God may be said to be further from the truth than our symbolic language, since the symbolic language is at one with the original language of the prophets and apostles, the eye- and ear-witnesses to revelation.

There is today an unhealthy skepticism concerning knowledge of God and the adequacy of human language to convey the mystery of God's self-revelation in Christ. I have already alluded to the skepticism of Pannenberg. Appealing to the Greek fathers, George Maloney argues that we can know something about God by reason alone, but we can never really know God except by wonder, since God is basically inexpressible and undefinable.[25] According to Gordon Kaufman, "*all* conceptions of God . . . including that of scripture and faith, must be understood as creations of the human imagination: the 'real God' is never available to us or directly knowable by us."[26] Gail Ramshaw-Schmidt says: "Human language cannot properly or adequately describe God."[27] In her opinion, a metaphor stretches the mind, but it says something radically other than what we want it to say. Virginia Mollenkott dismisses masculine images for God in the Bible as "simply symbols that the human imagination needs to fasten upon."[28] It seems that for many modern theologians, we are free to choose those symbols that best resonate with modern experience. If our language about God is only metaphorical, then when cultural experience changes we may readily alter the metaphors of faith, since metaphors are only tentative and exploratory, never final or definitive (McFague).

Thomas Torrance is one theologian who is duly disturbed by the rising epistemological skepticism in modern theology and philosophy. Far from being a rationalist, he acknowledges that "all true theological concepts and statements inevitably fall far short of the God to whom they refer."[29] At the same time, he insists that "there can be no knowledge of God, no faith, which is not basically conceptual or conceptual at its very root, and therefore there is no non-conceptual gap between God's revealing of himself and our knowing of him."[30] This does not mean that knowledge of God in his eternal being can be "captured within the grasp of our creaturely concepts," but it does mean "that the human concepts which arise in faith under the creative impact of the speech of God are grounded beyond themselves in the *ratio veritatis* of the divine Being."[31]

Against modern idealism and existentialism, Kenneth Hamilton contends that "the Word of God in the Old and New Testaments is never a symbolic word merely, but always an actual communication. It appears as an actual statement or command addressed to particular people at a particular time, and with a content that is to be understood quite objectively."[32] It is not basically emotive, but informative. Hamilton urges theologians to be on guard against both the empiricist reductionist approach to language, which ties meaning to univocity, and the idealistic-mystical approach, which seeks to get beyond words and concepts altogether.

Evangelical theology insists that a symbol does not simply point beyond itself to the ineffable but that it always contains a unity of meaning between the sign and the thing signified. This is not an identity, which would be the case in strict univocity, but a commonality. A symbol in the biblical sense yields conceptual knowledge, even propositional knowledge, though such knowledge remains broken and open-ended. The content of revelation is neither a symbol nor a nonsymbolic abstraction, but instead a divine act that is at the same time an announcement of redemption. Revelation is the act of God whereby something, as well as Someone, is revealed. We have the revelation of God in Christ clothed in the mythical imagery and symbolism of the biblical record, and this revelation is veiled, as well as revealed, through this symbolism.

Karl Barth is helpful in his contention that the divine content of revelation can never be divorced from its original symbolic garb—the language of Canaan or the language of Zion. The foundational symbols cannot be replaced, but they must be supplemented and interpreted. They cannot be replaced because they are based not on cultural experience but on a divine intrusion into cultural experience, a revelation that originates not in history or culture, but in eternity.

Even Paul Tillich, who dwelt on the need for resymbolizing the faith, admitted that the original words of revelation cannot be altered or replaced. Such a seminal word as *sin*, for example,

contains nuances of meaning that metaphors such as "alienation" and "estrangement" do not encompass. At the same
time, Tillich was adamant that all metaphors and symbols
must finally be transcended if we are to make contact with the
God above God, the undifferentiated unity behind the Trinity.

The Bible itself, it should be noted, does not so much
resymbolize as seek to interpret the symbols of culture and
religion in the light of the gospel, God's redemptive action in
history culminating in the life, death, and resurrection of Jesus
Christ. The symbols of religious tradition are not discarded,
but instead illumined by the revelatory acts of God in history.
Such words as *kairos* and *parousia,* derived from Hellenistic
philosophy and religion, are given a new meaning and
direction by the self-revelation of God in Jesus Christ.[33] Even
the seminal words of Hebraic religion such as *law, love,* and
peace, assumed a new thrust and content in the light of the
Christ revelation. The symbols of the Bible have a historical
rather than a mythical focus. Whereas myth dramatizes the
cycles of nature in terms of stories of gods and goddesses,
biblical religion historicizes the story of salvation so that it
becomes a celebration of what God has actually wrought in the
life history of his people. The biblical symbols cannot be
replaced, because the events of redemption cannot be dupli-
cated.

Paul Ricoeur says that the Bible gives us an indirect or
figurative presentation of the unconditional. I would rather
say that the Bible gives us a firsthand report of God's saving
deeds in history, a report that is often presented in symbolic
language but nevertheless deals with real happenings. It is not
the experience of the unconditional or of the New Being (as in
Tillich and Ricoeur), but the self-revelation of a personal and
living God that comprises the content and significance of holy
Scripture.

The biblical words are not merely ciphers of transcendence
(as in Jaspers and Buri), but graphic images that on the whole
mean what they say. This is to be understood, most often, not

in terms of literal identity, but in terms of a unity of meaning that faith alone can grasp. I here agree with Hendrikus Berkhof:

> When the symbolical terms function in the context to which they belong, they are so relevant and transparent that we may no longer say that they are used in a "figurative" sense. For then they share in the true analogy as it is grounded in the creation and actualized in the revelational encounter. When certain concepts are ascribed to God, they are thus not used figuratively but in their first and most original sense. God is not "as it were" a Father; he is the Father from whom all fatherhood on earth is derived.[34]

It is important to understand that it is not we who name God, but it is God who names himself by showing us who he is. In the Book of Exodus, God is described as "I am who I am" (Ex 3:14 NIV). He also reveals himself as Lord (*Adonai*), Jehovah (*Yahweh*), *Elohim,* and Father. In the New Testament, Jesus Christ is revealed as Lord (*Kyrios*) and Son, and the first person of the Trinity is called Father and *Abba* (dear Father). The names of God are God's self-designation of his person and being. Such names do not tell us who God is exhaustively, but they are informative symbols having a basis in revelation itself and therefore having binding authority on all who confess themselves as Christian.

In the Bible the name of God represents the very reality and being of God. It is in his name that he reveals himself and saves us.[35] "Our help is in the *name* of the Lord, who made heaven and earth" (Ps 124:8 RSV, italics mine). "And those who know Your name will put their trust in You" (Ps 9:10 NKJV). "You shall call his name Jesus, for he will save his people from their sins" (Mt 1:21 RSV). "And there is salvation in no one else, for there is no other name under heaven given among men by which we must be saved" (Acts 4:12 RSV). Jesus promised that wherever two or three were gathered together in his name, there would he be in the midst of them (Mt 18:20).

It is in the New Testament that we are first confronted with the Trinitarian name for God: Father, Son, and Spirit (Mt 28:19, 2 Cor 13:14). The mystery of the Trinity is inextricably associated with the mystery of the incarnation, for the Word that assumed flesh in Jesus was the same Word that preexisted with the Father in heaven and is made known by the interior witness of the Spirit. This Trinitarian symbol was impressed on the imagination of the apostolic church by the action of the Holy Spirit in awakening people to the messianic identity of Jesus. Robert Jenson convincingly maintains that Father, Son, and Spirit eventually came to occupy the same place in Christianity as Yahweh had occupied in the history of the people of Israel.[36]

The symbols of faith that compose the biblical witness have been elected by God as means of revelation and salvation. In the writing of Scripture the prophets and apostles were guided by the Spirit in their selection of certain foundational symbols and analogies that remain the criterion that guides as well as limits theological speculation. The biblical symbols constitute the parameters of theological thinking. These symbols and the content which they communicate must, of course, be related to religious and cultural experience throughout history. But we should interpret cultural life and experience in the light of the revelatory symbols of faith and not vice versa.

Behind the symbolism of faith is a metaphysical vision, and behind this vision is a divine revelation in actual history. The vision of faith rises out of the revelation, and the symbolism and language of faith are formed in the light of both this primal vision and the divine revelation.

What is given in revelation is not self-understanding as such or a true awareness of the unconditional, but instead an enduring perception of the will and purpose of God for us as believers and for the whole world. God reveals not only himself, but also his plan of salvation. He tells us not only who he is, but also what he demands from us as his people. We have this revelation primarily in the testimony of holy Scripture, though this original revelation is amplified and illumined in the tradition of the church. It can never be the possession of the church, however, since God always remains the subject of his revelation. The church must wait for the Spirit of God to disclose anew the truth of faith attested to but also hidden in the Scripture. In the critical period in which we live, it appears that the Spirit is revealing anew the Fatherhood of God and Lordship of Christ to a church that is increasingly falling under the spell of the mythologies and ideologies that mesmerize our culture.

THREE

God in Biblical Perspective

God Transcendent and Immanent

The God of the Bible is utterly transcendent but also radically immanent. He transcends the highest heaven (1 Kgs 8:27), and at the same time he is nearer to us than hands and feet (Augustine). He is primarily and originally transcendent and secondarily and derivatively immanent. That is to say, he exists prior to and independent of the creaturely world of time and change.[1] He created the world by the act of his will as something apart from him and yet wholly dependent on him. Historical theology has expressed this as *creatio ex nihilo* (creation out of nothing). This does not mean that he formed the world out of the nothingness of a preexistent chaotic matter, but instead that he called the worlds into being by his creative affirmation.

Karl Barth has described God as the Wholly Other (*totaliter aliter*), which expresses the infinite qualitative difference between time and eternity (Kierkegaard). This term might be regarded as a conceptual metaphor in that it should be taken not literally but symbolically. If taken literally, it would mean that God is totally dissimilar to man, and this would deny the doctrine of the *imago Dei*, that we are created in his image. It signifies that God is utterly beyond what the human imagina-

29

tion can conceive. It reminds us that we are separated from God both by ontological fate and by historical guilt. It is primarily because of our sin that we find God unapproachable and inaccessible. God is Wholly Other because he is the Holy One in whose presence we would be consumed as by a fire if we were not covered by the righteousness of Christ through justifying faith (cf. Is 6:4-7). The metaphor of Wholly Other was also used by Rudolf Otto[2] and is anticipated by comparable expressions in the heritage of Christian mysticism.[3]

In affirming the ontological transcendence of God, we must also make clear that God cannot be identified with anything creaturely, for this would be idolatry (Ex 20:4, 5; Dt 5:8, 9). The God of the Bible is not "the Man Upstairs" (cf. Nm 23:19; 1 Sm 15:29; Hos 11:9), a superindividual, but the creative source of all being. He might be described as the absolute, incomparable being—not in the sense of an isolated, absolute individual, but in the sense of an absolute participant. He is not a being alongside other beings, but the being who is the ground and center of all other things, the almighty Creator of all that exists. He can be considered "Being itself" or "the most really real" (*ens realissimum*), but these conceptual abstractions do not capture the personal and concrete reality of the living God, which the biblical metaphors and analogies reflect and describe. God is not simply being itself or the fullness of being, but Lord, Creator, Redeemer, and Father (cf. Is 63:16 RSV).

Besides being ontologically and epistemologically transcendent, the God of the Bible is radically immanent. He is not only the Creator-God, but the Eternal Spirit who is present to us and in us. He is not only the creative source of being but the sustainer of being. He is not only Creator but also protector, provider, and rejuvenator. The God of the Bible is diametrically opposed to the God of deism—the Eternal Clockmaker who stands aloof from his creation, removed from human concerns. This is a God who works within history and also upon history. He upholds humanity as well as intervenes in the affairs of humanity. Yet even when we come to discover this intimate relationship between God and humanity, we are always reminded of the infinite distance between them. God is eternal and therefore immortal; man is subject to disease and death. God is omnipotent and omniscient; man is limited both in power and in knowledge. God is dependable and holy; man is fickle and unholy.

The God of the Bible is monotheistic, but this is a trinitarian or concrete monotheism, not a mystical monotheism in which distinctions are swallowed up in a higher unity. To affirm God as a Trinity means that God not only exists as an absolute being, but also coexists as a fellowship within himself. He not only has the potentiality of love, but he also contains within himself the actual experience of love because he constitutes a community of persons in pure reciprocity. He does not need the world for fellowship because he has this fellowship of pure love within himself. Trinitarian monotheism affirms that there is one Subject interacting within itself in three ways, one divine consciousness in a threefold self-relatedness.[4]

While the Bible does not explicitly affirm the doctrine of the Trinity, this doctrine is an immediate implication of the fact, form, and content of divine revelation (Barth). It is already anticipated in the Old Testament where God is described as *Elohim* and *Adonai* (both indicating the plurality of majesty) and where God the Creator is distinguished and yet insepar- able from the divine wisdom and the divine Spirit. The three persons, Father, Son, and Holy Spirit are evident in the accounts of the baptism of Jesus (Mk 1:9-11; Mt 3:16, 17; Lk 3:21, 22), the great commission given by our Lord to his church (Mt 28:19; Acts 1:7, 8), and the last discourse of Christ with his disciples (Jn 15:1-27; 16:1-15). Unmistakable Trinitarian allusions are also to be found in the Pauline epistles where the apostle correlates the work of the Spirit, the Lord (Christ), and God (1 Cor 12:4-6; Eph 4:4-6; 2 Thes 2:13, 14; Gal 4:4-7; Rom 8:9-11; 2 Cor 13:14). The integral relationship between the Trinity and the incarnation is seen in John 1:1-18 where the Word is identified with God and yet distinguished from him.

Within the Trinity there is a certain dependence of the Son on the Father and of the Spirit on the Father and Son. The Father alone is unbegotten, whereas the Son is begotten (Jn 1:14, 18; 3:16, 18; 1 Jn 4:9 KJV). At the same time, the members of the Trinity enjoy an essential equality in that all participate in the activities of the others. Yet there is a difference in function and therefore a voluntary subordination. The Son subordinates himself to the Father, and the Spirit carries out the directives of the Father and the Son. Within this diversity there is an overarching unity. The church through the ages has confessed one being in three persons, meaning here not separate individuals (this would be Tritheism), but agencies of relationship. Because the meaning of person has changed from an abiding mode of being or activity (*hypostasis*) to an independent or autonomous individual, Karl Barth has rephrased the Trinitarian formula: there is one person in three modes of being. This is not modalism, however, because these three modes of being denote eternal distinctions within God himself and not simply ways by which God relates himself to the world.[5]

The doctrine of the Trinity is a mystery that escapes comprehension, and yet meaning shines through this mystery. It can be illuminated by metaphors drawn from human experience, such as water, steam, and ice, or the light, heat, and ionizing radiation of the one Sun. Here we see one substance in three dimensions or subsistences.

Significance of the Biblical Symbols

While the biblical witness is clear that the living God transcends sexuality, that he is neither male nor female, it is equally clear that he encompasses masculinity and femininity within himself. Indeed, we are created in his image as male and female (Gn 1:27; 5:1, 2). Masculinity and femininity are in God not univocally as in creatures, but in a more perfect way (*eminenter*).

God is not a man, but, for the most part, he chooses to relate himself to us as masculine. Yahweh, unlike the gods and goddesses of the pagan religions, has no consort. We, the church, are his consort, and this means that the church constitutes the feminine dimension of the sacred. Israel is portrayed in the Old Testament as the wife of Yahweh (Is 54:5; Hos 2:2, 7, 16) and the Daughter of Zion (Is 16:1; 62:11; Jer 6:2, 23; Lam 1:6; 2:18). The church is depicted as the bride of Christ in the new Testament. As Vernard Eller aptly puts it: "He has addressed us only as his beloved, only as feminine co-respondent to his own masculinity, not as confidant to his existence before the worlds began."[6]

Even feminist theologians reluctantly acknowledge that the language about God in the Bible is overwhelmingly masculine. While the Hebrew word for Spirit, *ruach*, is grammatically feminine in gender, its meaning is either neuter or masculine.[7] The adjective in Holy Spirit (*ruach qadosh*) is always masculine. If the feminine form of "holy" were used with *ruach*, it would probably indicate a cult prostitute. When Spirit is personified to mean Spirit of the Lord, the accompanying pronouns and possessive adjectives are consistently masculine. The modifying noun in "Spirit of your holiness" is also masculine (Ps 51:11; cf. Is 63:10). To assert on the basis of the feminine gender of *ruach* that the Bible therefore provides support for referring to the Holy Spirit as "she" and "her" shows a lack of both solid biblical scholarship and linguistic understanding. It also manifests an unfamiliarity with the fact that there is no necessary correlation between sex and gender in the Hebrew language.[8]

While the Greek word for Spirit, *pneuma*, is neuter, the primary thrust of the New Testament is to think of the Spirit as personal, and in virtually all contexts this means masculine. The Spirit can be blasphemed against (Mt 12:31, 32) and grieved (Eph 4:30). The pronouns and possessive adjectives for Spirit in John's Gospel are both neuter and masculine (cf. Jn 14:26; 15:26; 16:8).

This is not to imply, however, that feminine metaphors for God are totally absent in the Scriptures. In the Wisdom literature, Wisdom (*Hokmah*) is definitely portrayed as feminine and is referred to as both "Mother" and "Sister" (cf. Prv 7:4; Sir 24:18 RSV). In the New Testament, Wisdom is identified with Christ (Mt 11:19; 1 Cor 1:24). God is described in terms reminiscent of motherhood in Deuteronomy 32:11 (cf. Ps 131:2; Job 38:29). Isaiah on occasion employed female imagery to suggest the unfathomable love of God for his people (Is 49:14, 15; cf. 42:14; 66:13). Christ likens himself to a mother in Matthew 23: "How often would I have gathered your children together as a hen gathers her brood under her wings, and you would not!" (verse 37 RSV; cf. Lk 15:8-10). The motherly activity of the Spirit is suggested in John 3:5-8, where it is said that in order to enter the kingdom of God, one must be born of water and the Spirit (cf. Jn 1:13).

At the same time, although God is said to be like a mother, God is never called mother in the canonical Scriptures (though this is true of one apocryphal text), nor does mother ever occur in the vocative. The dominant names for God in the Bible and in the history of the church are *Deus, Domine,* and *Pater.* The God of the Bible is much closer to the Sky Father of prophetic religion than to the Earth Mother of the fertility religions. But the living God transcends and overcomes this polarity.

Nevertheless, because feminine as well as masculine imagery for God exists in the Scriptures, it is possible to speak of a divine motherhood as well as a divine fatherhood. Yet the latter is the controlling symbol. Femininity is grounded in mascu-

linity in the Bible (Eve came out of Adam) just as motherhood
is grounded in fatherhood. The masculine is the ground of the
feminine, but the feminine is the goal and glory of the
masculine (1 Cor 11:7).

When we speak of God as Father in the biblical sense, it
should be borne in mind that this is not a mere symbol.
Theologians of such diverse persuasions as Thomas Aquinas,
Hendrikus Berkhof, Karl Barth, and Thomas Torrance are
unanimous that when Father refers to God, especially in the
context of devotion, the word is not figurative, but closer to
being literal in that it is practically transparent to what it
signifies. The same can be said about Jesus Christ when he is
called Son and Lord. Yet this cannot be made to apply to the
reference to Jesus as Good Shepherd or the True Vine. These
are metaphors drawn from cultural experience that illumine
and at the same time veil the mystery of the divinity of Christ.
Yet to call upon him by the name *Jesus* or to confess him as
Lord is to use a much more precise designation.

Such words as Father, Son, and Lord, when applied to God,
are analogies, but they are analogies *sui generis*. They are
derived not from the experience of human fatherhood or
sonship or lordship, but from God's act of revealing himself as
Father, Son, and Lord.[9] They are therefore more accurately
described as *catalogies* than analogies insofar as they come
from above.

We come to know the meaning of true fatherhood and true
lordship when we realize that God is our heavenly Father and
that Christ is our divine Lord. These might indeed be
considered as transformational images in that they drastically
alter the ordinary or cultural understanding of these terms. It
is not that God resembles a Father, but in calling him Father
the Bible challenges the human view of what a father should
be.[10] The same is true for depictions of God as Judge, Lord,
Savior, and Son.

It is theologically more appropriate to see these basic

appellations for God as primal symbols rather than root metaphors. A metaphor has its basis in cultural experience and only imperfectly describes the reality to which it points. To speak of God metaphorically often verges on equivocation. But Father, Son, and Holy Spirit are symbols corresponding not to inner feelings or experiences, but to ontological realities. Their dominant reference is objective rather than subjective. They are hierarchical and organic symbols, not male images. Robert Roth rightly observes: "When we call God Father we do not ascribe to him masculine attributes. This word has a host of new meanings when it refers to God."[11]

To put this another way, the Trinitarian names are ontological symbols based on divine revelation rather than personal metaphors having their origin in cultural experience. They refer to a threefold self-relatedness within God rather than to human or societal relationships. "The terms 'son' and 'father,'" says Torrance, "carry a creaturely content with which we are familiar in the interrelations between a human father and a human son, and as such they may not be read back into the inner relations of God's own Being."[12] A case can nonetheless be made that these terms, "inadequate as they are in themselves, point ostensively to real relations in God beyond themselves, since they are economically rooted in God's own *self*-giving and *self*-revealing in Jesus Christ and are therefore ultimately real and valid in God as well as for us."[13]

Robert Roth offers an insightful explanation of why biblical faith prefers to conceive of God as masculine rather than feminine:

One reason for the appropriateness of the Father metaphor in biblical revelation is the aggressive surprise of time as against the repetition of nature. Creation does not arise out of a matrix; redemption does not naturally emerge from a womb. Grace is given and the creature is receptive to the action of the giver. The amazing thing about grace is that it comes from above, not from within, and that it therefore brings freedom from fate.[14]

Paul Ricoeur, the hermeneutical theologian, reminds us that Yahweh, the God of the Old Testament, is not only designated as "Father," but declared to be *the* Father. Our Lord declared: "Call no man your father on earth, for you have one Father, who is in heaven" (Mt 23:9 RSV). According to Ricoeur, Jesus' sonship is not set out in analogy to the sons of earthly fathers. True Fatherhood as well as true Sonship is grounded in the new Testament understanding of God as the Father and Jesus Christ as his Son.

The masculine symbolism for the divine in the Bible is not sufficient, however, without the corresponding feminine symbolism that completes the divine activity. The masculine refers to the movement of God going out of himself to other members of the Trinity and to the world. Here we see creativeness, initiative, and aggressiveness. The feminine refers to the movement of God returning to himself in the role of the Spirit embodied in the church. Here we see receptivity, openness, spontaneity, intuitiveness. Femininity is not to be equated, however, with passivity and servility. As Forsyth says: "Our cooperation with God is our receptivity; but it is an active, a laborious receptivity, an importunity that drains our strength away if it does not tap the sources of the Strength Eternal."[15]

God going out of himself and returning to himself is not to be understood in Platonic or Neoplatonic terms. I am referring to God in his acts of creation and redemption as well as his act of the ingathering of souls, the return of the Prodigal to the Father. The divine fatherhood, therefore, includes the divine motherhood. God not only creates and begets but also gives birth and nurtures as a mother or nurse. But this motherly activity is seen in the church where children of faith are born. The motherhood of God is mirrored in the church, which should be viewed not simply as a social institution but as the body of Christ, the temple of God, the vessel or bearer of the glory of God, the *Shekinah*. The church might also be understood as the historical embodiment of the Holy Spirit who brings people into a saving relationship with Christ and transforms them in the Father's image. If we are to follow the biblical way, we will designate God as our Father and the church as our Mother.[16] We refer to the motherhood of God indirectly when we call the church "our Holy Mother." There is a divine side to the church as well as a human side, and we Protestants, especially, have lost sight of this dimension of the sacred by thinking of the church primarily and essentially as a gathered body of believers.

In writing on prayer, Tertullian associated the church with both Father and Son:

> The title of Father expresses veneration and power. At the same time, the Son is invoked in the Father. . . . But mother Church is not forgotten either. In the Father and the Son, one recognizes the Mother, by whom the name of the Father like that of the Son is guaranteed.[17]

The Catholic devotional writer Madeleine Delbrêl describes the intimate relation between believers and their spiritual mother: "I am his—in the [Holy Catholic] church. I am in her as a cell in a living body. She transmits to me the life of the children of God."[18]

In the catholic heritage of the church, Mary too has come to personify and exemplify the divine motherhood. Mary indeed is a type of the church, and such an understanding has solid biblical support (cf. Rv 12). Mary said to the angel: "Let it be to me according to your word" (Lk 1:38 NKJV). Here we see the essence of femininity in the biblical sense: fidelity, servanthood, meekness. This last is not to be construed as weakness, but on the contrary, as boldness and resoluteness. In their relationship to God and Christ, all Christians are called to assume the role of the feminine.

Goddess Religion

It should be remembered that the chief threat to biblical faith was in the goddess religion of the fertility cults of the ancient Near East. The goddess was not so much a focus of personhood as a symbol of the mystery of fecundity. The goddesses did not rule alone but often had male consorts. Even when the male gods were elevated and seemed to be supreme, it was clear that ultimacy was still ascribed to the Earth Mother.[19]

The biblical prophets were adamant that there could be no synthesis with this type of religion but only exclusion and replacement. Their stance was based not on a commitment to patriarchy (the devotees of the goddess were even more stringently patriarchal than the people of Israel), but on a steadfast resolve to remain true to the basic vision of their faith that God revealed himself as sovereign Lord, as *one* and as the *only* God.

How different today are feminist theologians, who rush to incorporate the values of the goddess religions. Rosemary Ruether, standing in the mainstream of reformist feminism, contends that we must allow Canaanite religion to criticize Hebrew religion if we are to find an alternative to sexism.[20] She proposes a synthesis of Canaanite goddess religion and Hebraic prophetic religion. No wonder that she thinks of God primarily as "God/ess" or Primal Matrix rather than Jehovah God or Father God.

It is often argued by feminists that to challenge the strict monotheism of biblical faith means to overthrow patriarchy and prepare the way for an egalitarian, holistic society. Yet it can be shown that the goddess religions of the Near East were far more oppressively patriarchal than Hebraic religion. Indeed, women were able to gain a real place of stature in Hebraic religion, even though the patriarchal culture was still intact. On the other hand, women were often held in low esteem in the cultures dominated by the fertility cults. Regarding the mother goddess in Babylon, for example, "though the dominant metaphor in this cult is feminine, it is dedicated to a view of woman which reduces her to a sex object, thereby thrusting life into a debased one-dimensionality."[21] Martin Buber, the eminent Jewish philosopher, remarks that the chief danger to prophetic religion came from the mother goddesses, posing a threat not only to the purity of the faith, but also to the humanity of women. "For in a religion," he says, "in which the inherent dynamism of nature is worshipped as the force which procreates life, and always more life, women are inevitably considered as only fulfilling a sexual role."[22] Gnostic religion, too, which was remarkably open to feminine metaphors for the divine, did little or nothing to advance the role of women in society.[23]

Modern feminist theology and religion signifies a resurgence of ancient goddess spirituality. Merlin Stone argues that the core and motivational energy of the feminist movement is goddess spirituality which, "in all of its aspects . . . has grown from our continually feeling, speaking, comparing, analyzing, feminist-consciousness-raising process . . . it has grown from US. It may be the ultimate heresy—and it may ultimately be what allows us to succeed where so many others have failed."[24]

Far from being the outcome of a patriarchal culture, Yahwist religion proved to be a transformation of patriarchy. While patriarchal symbols were used to represent God, these symbols were drastically transformed. Christianity challenged autocratic patriarchy by putting human fatherhood in second place. Cultural ideas of lordship were also transformed, for Christ chose to realize his lordship in the role of a servant (Mt 20:25-28; Lk 22:24-27). At the same time, God chose to reveal himself in a patriarchal society, perhaps because patriarchy preserves the biblical principle of an above and below, a before and after, a first and second. To deny or erase the distinctions between the members of the Trinity or between God and man or between man and woman is to end in a pantheistic monism in which creaturehood is swallowed up in deity.

Goddess spirituality is a perennial temptation in the life of the church, but it must be firmly rejected, for it challenges the basic intuitions of faith—that God is Lord and King of all creation, that the world was created by divine fiat rather than formed from the being of God as an emanation of God, that God utterly transcends sexuality. Whenever biblical theism is threatened by philosophical monism, whether this takes the form of pantheism or panentheism, theologians must be vigilant in reaffirming the biblical principle of the infinite qualitative difference between God and the world (cf. Is 40:6-8; 55:8, 9; 1 Kgs 8:27; Ecc 5:2) and the absolute sovereignty of God over his creation (Is 40:12-17; 45:7; 64:8; Prv 21:1; Job 38, 39).

FOUR

Resymbolizing the Faith

The Grammar of Feminism

Besides the various committees at work on the revision of hymnals and prayer books, many book publishers, newspapers, and magazines, secular as well as religious, are capitulating to feminist demands for a nonsexist language about God. At first glance, some of the substitute terms do not appear to be offensive, but a close examination reveals that the traditional understanding of God has undergone a disturbing metamorphosis.

Suggestions for new language concerning the first person of the Trinity are abundant. Some propose speaking of God as "Heavenly Parent" rather than "Heavenly Father," but this is to depersonalize God. Others such as the NCC Lectionary Committee advocate speaking of God as "Father/Mother" or "Father and Mother." Rosemary Ruether proposes the metaphor "God/ess." But all these terms signify an androgynous interpretation of God and are closer to being binitarian than Trinitarian. It means that the triad has been replaced by a dyad. Gail Ramshaw-Schmidt rightly objects that such language tends to portray God as a hermaphrodite. Yet her own substitute, "the Fatherly One," does not have the intimacy associated with "Heavenly Father" or even less with the "dear Father" (*Abba*) of Jesus.[1]

Radical feminists have no hesitation in referring to God as

43

Mother, but this in effect transmutes God into a goddess. At the Presbytery conference on this subject at which I was speaking, I was asked by a laywoman, "What is wrong with the idea of a goddess?" The answer is that such a metaphor imputes sexuality to a God who is beyond sexuality. It also denies the transcendence of God, since goddess invariably refers to the Immanent Mother, the creative force within nature. One feminist scholar acknowledges that a shift in symbolism from God the Father to a Mother Goddess means a new religion:

> The symbolism of the Goddess is not a parallel structure to the symbolism of God the Father. The Goddess does not rule the world; She *is* the world. Manifest in each of us, She can be known internally by every individual, in all her magnificent diversity.[2]

Among the new symbols or images for God the Father presented in feminist literature are "Womb of Being," "Primal Matrix," "Immanent Mother," feminine "Life-force," "Creatrix," "God/ess," "the divine Generatrix," "Eternal Spirit," "Shalom of the Holy," "the empowering Matrix," and "ground of being." A liturgical manual of the United Church of Christ even contains a prayer addressed to the Ground of Being.[3] The trouble with this term, as well as the others mentioned above, is that it is not equivalent to the biblical language where God is portrayed in a more realistic fashion. Such metaphors as "Womb of Being" and "Primal Matrix" (both favored by Rosemary Ruether) simply do not encompass the meanings associated with heavenly Father, *Adonai,* and *Yahweh.* Indeed, they bear a closer resemblance to Asherah, Isis, and Gaia, ancient mythological deities symbolizing the Earth Mother.

Some revisionists seek to resurrect the language of Deism: Divine Providence, Source of Sustenance, and Cosmic Benefactor. But these terms definitely portray a God who is remote and removed from the trials and agonies of the world. Others look to the language of process philosophy: Creative Process, Divine Eros, Creativity, Directive of History, Absolute Relatedness, Creative Transformation, Creative Event, Principle of Concretion, and Growth in Qualitative Meaning. The question is: Can we pray to gods with such names? The process theologian Henry Nelson Wieman insisted that God is not a person because creativity is prior to personality. This means that prayer then takes the form of meditation and reflection on the creative powers within nature; any idea of supplication to a personal God who hears and answers prayer is no longer possible.[4]

There is also a move in those circles influenced by feminist theology to do away with masculine pronouns and adjectives. Instead of referring to God as "He," feminist ideologues suggest simply repeating the word God. Rather than saying "God himself," they recommend "God in essence" or "God-self." In my contribution to a book of essays on Scripture, the original text contained the words "God himself reveals." The publisher's copy editor changed this to "God is revealed." Another suggestion that the company would have accepted is "what is revealed by God." Needless to say, I asked that the original wording be restored because the change in language also entailed a change in meaning. A God who reveals himself is not the same as a God who is revealed by something or someone else. It is the difference between an active, living God and a God who is passive and unmoved.

Revisionists are also searching for new language for the second person of the Trinity. It is considered bad taste to refer to Christ as "Lord" or "King," since these are hierarchical words, indicating domination and subjection. In place of such offensive designations, they propose such words as "Friend" and "Child." The NCC Lectionary gives this rendering of Matthew 11:27: "All things have been delivered to me by [*God*] my Father [*and Mother*]; and no one knows the *Child* except *God*, and no one knows *God* except the *Child* and any one to whom the *Child* chooses to reveal *God*" (italics mine).[5] Besides the singularly awkward style, this alteration can be faulted for obscuring the intra-Trinitarian relation between the Son and the Father. Moreover, the metaphor "Child" carries the connotation of immaturity and lacks the sublimity of "Son" and "Lord."

An even more grievous departure from the faith is to be found in the NCC Lectionary reading for John 1:14, which refers to "the only Child" of "the Father and Mother." Here there is an obvious change in meaning in which a polytheistic or mythological picture of the Godhead gains ascendance over biblical monotheism.

The term "Sovereign One," which the NCC Lectionary offers as a substitute for "Lord," indicates another move away from the personal and anthropomorphic to the suprapersonal. It even suggests the suprapersonal "One" of Neoplatonic mysticism, the "God above God" of Plotinus, Dionysius, Valentinus, and Tillich. Marjorie Suchocki, who combines feminist and process theology, frankly declares that God should be named the "One," for "it is the single unity of God" that accounts for the living symphony of the divine life in the world.[6] Yet, in her perspective this One is not the absolute simplicity of Neoplatonism, but the dynamic harmony and unity of all possibilities.

In place of "the Son of Man," which is considered too masculine, the NCC Lectionary speaks of "the Human One." Here again we see how an alteration in root symbols also entails a transformation in meaning. The "Son of Man" is an honorific title indicating a supernatural being, whereas "the Human One" is a model of authentic selfhood.

Some advocate thinking of Christ as the Daughter of the Father, since the Son or Word is supposedly born in the bosom of the Father. Susan Thistlethwaite appeals to the Third Council of Toledo in maintaining that the procession of the Son from the Father is both a male and a female action. The Council asserted "that the Son was created neither out of nothingness nor yet out of any substance, but that He was begotten or born out of the Father's womb (*de utero Patris*), that is, out of His very essence."[7] Yet this is patently metaphorical rather than literal language, and to press this metaphor is to sexualize the relationship between God and Christ, a throwback to mythological religion. Paul Jewett rightly reminds us that the doctrine of the virgin birth tells us that not only did Jesus have no earthly father, but he also had no heavenly Mother (in contradistinction to surrounding pagan religion).[8]

The identification of Christ with Wisdom, on the other hand, has solid biblical foundation, and this is why a tradition within the church has portrayed Christ as Mother in his relation to us. Julian of Norwich occasionally called Christ "our Mother," though she was careful always to refer to the first person of the Trinity as "Father." I believe that Christ in his role as Wisdom who nurtures and guides the people of God can be thought of as feminine, but Christ in his role as Lord and Savior of the world, Christ in his inseparable relationship to Jesus, must always be envisaged as masculine.

It is the third person of the Trinity that is most often referred to by feminine appellations. John Dart, among others, advocates calling the Holy Spirit "she," though still referring to Christ and God as "he." "A case could be made," he says, "that a female Holy Spirit represents an important early teaching of Jesus' followers."[9] While there is assuredly a feminine dimension to the activity of the Spirit, to posit an abiding feminine principle within a basically masculine God-head is to bifurcate the Trinity and to make God bisexual. Gail Ramshaw-Schmidt complains that this approach conjures in the imagination the picture of a heavenly family up in the air. Zinzendorf was accustomed to refer to the Holy Spirit as "Mother," though this was never made into a rule. As I see it, the Spirit as the soul of the church can be thought of as feminine, but the Spirit in his regenerating and sanctifying action on the people of God is properly portrayed as masculine.

Gnostic Resymbolizing

It is well to keep in mind that the first major attempt to resymbolize the faith was carried on by the Christian Gnostics in the first several centuries of the church.[10] In his penetrating study of this phenomenon, Samuel Laeuchli documents how the mother principle infiltrated into the meaning of God's fatherhood among the Gnostics:

The parallelism between Father and Mother seems at first harmless, almost poetic. As time passes, it reaches the full-fledged realm of fertility religion. Beside God steps a mother deity. Christ becomes the son of a "Mother of life." The . . . Gnostics do not hesitate to adore this mother principle. "Mother" has become a primal deity, "the mother of all creatures," to which one prays and in whose name the blessing is said.[11]

In Gnostic speculation the Father principle was understood no longer vertically, theologically, in the father-son relationship but now biologically, in the father-mother relation.[12] God as Father of Israel began to lose his uniqueness and sovereignty as he was ever more associated with the biological, generative realm. No longer the one Lord of his people, he was now envisaged as one of two, three, or many.

With the transmutation of God's Fatherhood from the theological to the biological realm, the concept could no longer be ultimate for the Gnostics. This is why they pressed for a God beyond Fatherhood—an "Eternal Silence" or "Primal Ground" or "Incomprehensible One." None of the names concocted by the human imagination (such as Father, Lord, and Son) are fitting for this God,[13] they said, since he is "the totally different, the other, the unknown."[14]

While there was a certain reluctance to discard the biblical symbols, their meaning was transformed in the light of more ultimate symbols. Gnosticism proved to be an excursus religion calling people into a new faith orientation—a kind of syncretistic mysticism in which the unique claims of biblical faith were compromised and subverted.

Laeuchli points to the profound differences between the language of Gnosticism and of biblical faith:

> Gnostic language lacks the salient directions of biblical language. The language of God and man is bereft of its one purpose, to express man in confrontation with God, God coming to man in Christ. The communication of an encounter turns into a communication of "nature"—either the nature of heaven (cosmogony), or the nature of Christ (his coming down through the angelic spheres), or the nature of man (dualism). Language about Israel, *ekklesia*, and time is replaced by language embracing heaven, pneuma, and time. The communication of events on earth in their relation to God turns into the communication of theosophy forced into dualistic and monistic frames. The faith-love-hope complex is overpowered by gnosis. Ethical language is not absent but erratic; hope is spiritualized like all other eschatological language in the Bible; faith, the key word in Paul, has been completely conquered by knowledge, the saving *mysterion*. The language of faith has become the language of knowledge.[15]

Just as the Christian Gnostics brought to the faith of the church the ontology and metaphysics of their age, so well-meaning Christians bring to the church of today a metaphysics alien to the thought world of Scripture. The study of theology invariably involves a clash between two languages. The church of our time, like the church in the patristic period, must struggle to maintain the integrity of the canonical language in the face of the new monisms and dualisms that pervade modern culture. It is not simply a question of maintaining the personal character of God, but of remaining faithful to the metaphysical and spiritual vision of the biblical and apostolic community of faith.

The Problem of Inclusive Language

While the language of faith should be as inclusive as the gospel itself, problems arise when people motivated by ideological commitment seek to improve upon the language of revelation. First of all, it has to be shown that the biblical terms "Father, Son, and Holy Spirit" exclude women and children from a meaningful role in the life of the church. I have argued that Fatherhood in the biblical context includes motherhood, and Sonship encompasses certain nuances of meaning associated with daughters. Jesus Christ, though admittedly in male form, represents all of humankind, men and women. It is fallacious to argue (as do some feminists) that he took on impersonal humanity rather than the specific humanity of the man Jesus, for this is to deny the real incarnation in human flesh. The feminine dimension of the Son is to be located in the Godhead itself, since the Son is equated with Wisdom, who is feminine in relation to the Father as his helpmate in creation, and who exercises a motherly and sisterly role in relation to the people of God.

It is now customary in mainline Protestant churches to replace the Trinitarian formula "Father, Son, and Holy Spirit" with "Creator-Redeemer-Sustainer" or something similar. Other proposed substitutes are "Shepherd-Helper-Refuge" and "God-Christ-Spirit."[16] I agree with the Advisory Council on Discipleship and Worship in the Presbyterian Church (USA) that the traditional formula "speaks to who God is," whereas the substitutes are generally "functional terms describing what the Triune God does." The report continues:

The history of trinitarian doctrine makes plain that the church could not so separate the works of the Trinity as though it were only the Father who creates, only the Son who redeems, and only the Spirit who sustains and sanctifies.... Rather, it is the triune God (Father-Son-Holy Spirit) who is the Creator, Redeemer, and Sustainer. To say less if to jettison the personal character of the Christian confession for a vague and general monotheism.[17]

We should also heed these timely words of Harold Nebelsick, professor of theology at Louisville Presbyterian Theological Seminary:

It takes but a preliminary introduction to the doctrine of the Trinity to make one realize that "God" is not the equivalent of "Father." Further, "Christ" is Greek for the Hebrew "Messiah." The understanding of "Christ" is integral to the Christian understanding of "the Son" as the second person of the Trinity, but it is in no sense the equivalent of, or substitute for, "son" in Trinitarian understanding. Rather, the Trinitarian formula from the time of the formulation of the doctrine through the writing of our latest confessional documents is *God* the Father, *God* the Son, and *God* the Holy Spirit. It is a unity in threeness in which each of the three persons, at one and the same time, has his own particularity and each is fully and wholly God.[18]

To replace the foundational symbolism of faith with more inclusive symbolism such as Creator, Redeemer, and Sustainer is to abandon the ontological or essential Trinity for the economic Trinity, in which the three terms refer only to a threefold activity of God and not also to a threefold relationship within himself. This is the ancient heresy of modalism associated with the theologian Sabellius, who was willing to affirm that God assumes three roles, but not that he is in himself Father, Son, and Spirit.

Lutheran theologian Martha Stortz also has grave reservations concerning the move toward more inclusive language about God.[19] She is especially critical of Letty Russell's suggestion that we think of the Trinity as "Creator, Christ, and Spirit." In her opinion, "'Creator' does not indicate the vastness of the Father's work; 'Redeemer' does not embrace the breadth of the Son's work; 'Sanctifier' is not the sum of the Spirit's work."[20] She goes on to point out where the transformation in symbolism inevitably leads:

> It would be easy for a "Creator" to sacrifice a "Christ." Perhaps the category "sacrifice" would not even apply. It is not so easy for a Father to sacrifice a Son. Yet this is the story of our faith. We could choose another story—Creator, Christ, and Spirit; the Mother, the Son, and the Bullrushes—but then we would have to choose another faith and another confession of that faith.[21]

The proposed alterations in the Trinitarian formula have drastic practical implications for the liturgy and life of the church. Invocations and benedictions are now being said in the name of the Father-Mother God or in the name of Creator, Redeemer, and Sustainer. Baptisms are being performed in the new inclusive language rather than in "the name of the Father and of the Son and of the Holy Spirit." What is glaringly apparent is that a creeping unitarianism and binitarianism are edging out historical Trinitarianism.

Such phraseology as Creator, Redeemer, and Sanctifier (or Sustainer) has biblical warrant, and it is therefore not questionable in and of itself. Indeed, it indicates that the God we worship is wider and deeper than the Trinitarian names can of themselves convey. As supplements to the traditional formula, these terms have an honorable place, even in liturgy. But when they become substitutes for the Trinitarian names (especially in the rite of baptism), we are headed for a new religion. They are then in the service of heterodoxy because they indicate an economic and not an ontological Trinity. When God is described primarily in terms of function rather than of organic personal relationship, this may very well be a sign of the resurgence of the ancient heresy of modalism.

At the same time, I think we need to be alive to the concern of women for wider acknowledgment of the feminine dimension of the sacred. The God of the Bible is not exclusively masculine, nor is he exclusively monarchical. He is not only Lord but also Friend, not only Father and Brother but also Mother and Sister. We need to be open to a certain amount of experimentation that does not deny or ignore the biblical fact that God chooses to relate himself to us primarily in the masculine gender. On the other hand, we must not fall into the error of Virginia Mollenkott, who contends that the relationship between God and ourselves is one of "mutuality," "reciprocity," and "parallelism."[22] This denies that God is over us and above us before he is with us and for us. God is friend, to be sure, but he is Master before he is friend (as even Whitehead acknowledged).

While we should refrain from altering the language of public worship in any basic way (until the church as a whole speaks with an unequivocal voice on this issue), we can afford to be more flexible in the language of private devotions. Anselm offered this prayer: "And you Jesus, are you not also a mother? Are you not the mother who like a hen gathers her children under her wings?"[23] I would propose prayers such as the following, which would not be out of place even in public worship: "Dear God, heavenly Father, you who are also our mother, brother, sister, and friend. . . ."; and "Most Gracious God, Creator and Father of us all, You who are like a mother and sister as well as a father and brother. . . ." Here we see that the controlling symbol is still God the Father, and the motherhood and sisterhood of God are therefore seen in relation to this primal symbol.

Gail Ramshaw-Schmidt believes that we can experiment in liturgical prayer within certain parameters. She offers this prayer for our consideration: "O God, you are a nursing mother to all your faithful people. Nourish us with the milk of your word that we may live and grow in you, through your Son Jesus Christ our Lord."[24] Her motivation, she says, is "to follow scriptural metaphors rather than cultural suggestions in determining the use of feminine images." I have no fundamental objection to this particular prayer as such and regard it as a Christian prayer. Yet I believe that this kind of innovation needs general ratification by the councils of the wider church before it can be officially introduced in public worship. I firmly believe that no church body should act on its own on matters such as this without consultation with other churches, including the Roman Catholic and Eastern Orthodox churches.

I have heard of communion services where the benediction was offered "in the name of our Elder Sister" rather than the Triune God. This kind of innovation reveals a break with tradition in the direction of goddess spirituality. We must be extremely careful, particularly in a time when biblical monotheism is being challenged by naturistic mysticism and other forms of immanentalism. We also need to be consistent in our use of metaphors and images in devotion, both public and private. To switch from the masculine to the feminine in our descriptions of God in a service of worship is inevitably to present a false picture of God—a deity who is bisexual or androgynous rather than one who transcends the polarity of the sexes. Another possible and equally unsatisfactory alternative is to think of God as an impersonal or suprapersonal ground of being, as do Christian Scientists who generally address God as Mother-Father. Even in personal devotions, we need to exercise caution, since it is very probable that the habit of addressing God sometimes as Father and sometimes as Mother would finally lead to conceiving God as suprapersonal or impersonal, rather than personal. Yet this does not mean that on occasion, especially in our private devotions, we cannot address God as "Holy Mother, Wisdom of God" or something similar, for such usage has a measure of support, not only in the Bible, but also in orthodox church tradition.[25]

We need to keep in mind a fact particularly unpalatable to the modern ethos: Christian faith is not only inclusive but also exclusive. God revealed himself only to a particular people, the children of Israel, though the fruits of this revelation are intended for all of humanity. He incarnated himself in the person of Jesus Christ, a man who lived and died in a particular time and place. In the person of Jesus Christ he acted to redeem the whole world of its sins, and yet this redemption is effectual only for those who have faith. He designated himself as Father, Son, and Holy Spirit and thereby excluded other designations, particularly those associated with goddess spirituality and the fertility cults. He announced that there is only one way to salvation, namely, faith in Jesus Christ, and that if we try to get into the kingdom by other doors we will be thrown out (cf. Mt 22:11-14; Jn 10:1-5). His desire is that none of humanity should perish (cf. Ez 18:23, 32; 2 Pt 3:9), but his foreknowledge is that only some of humanity will believe. He is Lord of all creation but Savior only of the church. The exclusivistic and particularistic claims of the gospel are stumbling blocks to people today, especially in our democratic, egalitarian culture that is distrustful of making distinctions between people. It could be that the shift toward a more inclusive language for God is motivated partly by an ideological or cultural bias that envisions a one-world community characterized by liberty, equality, and fraternity, a kingdom of freedom brought about by social engineering, rather than a kingdom of heaven to be inaugurated by divine intervention and presaging the collapse and overthrow of the kingdoms of this world.

FIVE

The Problem of Authority

Authority in Feminism

Feminists are surprisingly united, not only in the area of goals, but also in their understanding of authority. For nearly all feminists, the final court of appeal is human experience, particularly feminine experience.

Rosemary Ruether is typical in this regard: "Human experience is the starting point and the ending point of the hermeneutical circle. Codified tradition both reaches back to roots in experience and is constantly renewed or discarded through the test of experience."[1] Although making a place for revelation, she sees this not as a supernatural communication of information about God through historical events or even directly to the human soul, but instead as a breakthrough into a higher level of consciousness or as a new awareness of self and the world. Revelatory experiences are "breakthrough experiences beyond ordinary fragmented consciousness that provide interpretive symbols illuminating . . . the *whole* of life."[2] The ultimate never intrudes as a foreign element into experience but is in fact a dimension of all experience.

Ruether sees an underlying affinity between feminist and liberation theologies: both have their genesis in the experience of oppression, and both seek a world free from exploitation.

"In rejecting androcentrism (males as norms of humanity)," she says, "women must also criticize all other forms of chauvinism: making white Westerners the norm of humanity, making Christians the norm of humanity, making privileged classes the norm of humanity."[3]

The more radical feminists are inclined to have a mystical criterion for faith, reflecting a monistic rather than a dualistic world view. (The mainstream feminists are also closer to monism than to dualism, but they draw back from pantheism). What is decisive is not human experience as such but making contact with the deepest within human experience—the creative powers within nature. Meinrad Craighead calls for a religion "connected to the metamorphoses of nature: the pure potential of water, the transformative power of blood, the seasonal rhythms of the earth, the cycles of lunar dark and light."[4] Charlene Spretnak states that "the worldview inherent in feminist spirituality is, like the female mind, holistic and integrative. We see *connectedness* where the patriarchal mentality insists on seeing only separations."[5] In the words of Starhawk, "Justice is not based on an external Absolute who imposes a set of laws upon chaotic nature, but on recognition of the ordering principles inherent in nature. The law is the natural law."[6] In fact, for her: "Individual conscience—itself a manifestation of the Goddess—is the final court of appeals, above codified laws or hierarchical proclamations."[7]

Obviously, men who embrace the cause of feminism do not appeal to feminine experience, nor are they as inclined to celebrate the cycles of nature. Instead, their authority is the new consciousness of living in a male-female world, a world in which hierarchy and duality are replaced by mutuality and unity.

Both men and women in the feminist orbit align themselves with the cultural vision of a holistic humanity characterized, not by separation between the sexes, but by an androgynal unity. The norms for feminism are therefore cultural rather than ecclesiastical, experiential rather than biblical.

The Bible in Feminism

This is not to deny that the Bible has a role (sometimes important) among Christian feminists, though it is not the ruling norm but an aid in bringing to people a new horizon of meaning. It is treated not as an inspired witness to a unique and definitive revelation of God in the history of the people of Israel culminating in Jesus Christ, but as an illuminating record of the struggles of the people of Israel for liberation from political and economic enslavement.

Elisabeth Schüssler-Fiorenza contends that only those parts of the Bible that lend support to the struggle for liberation should be accepted as authoritative. She calls for a "depatriarchalizing" of the Bible in which we interpret the Bible in the light of a canon within the canon. Those passages promoting equality between the sexes and races become the norm by which we weigh the validity of other parts of the Bible. For, she argues, "only the nonsexist and non-androcentric traditions of the Bible and the nonoppressive traditions of biblical interpretation have the theological authority of revelation if the Bible is not to continue as a tool for the oppression of women."[8] Thus the paradigm of "emancipatory praxis" is the criterion or norm for biblical interpretation.[9] The Bible is to be understood not as an archetype but as a prototype—"one critically open to the possibility, even the necessity of its own transformation."[10]

Reflecting the influence of David Tracy, Sallie McFague asserts that "the authority of Scripture is the authority of a classic poetic text."[11] Therefore "its interpretation is flexible," meaning that "the world it presents is open to different understandings."[12] The Bible is to be seen as "great literature" rather than a document of divine revelation. "The Bible as model," she says, "can never *be* the word of God, can never capture the ways of God. As model, the Bible can never be an idol. As poetic classic, the Bible continues, as does any great poetic work, to speak universally."[13] It should be interpreted "as other poetic texts are interpreted—existentially, flexibly, openly."[14] She emphasizes "the relative, groping character of this very human work" rather than its inspiration and canonicity.[15]

Most radical feminists do not hesitate to disavow the Bible either as a means to discover the reality of God or as an aid in the struggle for women's liberation. Carol Christ says bluntly that the "symbol systems cannot simply be rejected, they must be replaced. Where there is not any replacement, the mind will revert to familiar structures."[16] For Naomi Goldenberg, witchcraft is "the only Western religion that recognizes woman as a divinity in her own right."[17] Rita Gross suggests that we enrich our imagery of female divinity by meditating on the Hindu goddesses.[18]

Feminists on the left of the ideological spectrum who make a place for the Bible generally emphasize its insufficiency as a norm for faith and conduct because of its roots in a patriarchal culture. Sister Ann Patrick Ware, former associate director of the Commission on Faith and Order of the National Council of Churches, contends that the Word of God "is in need of correction," since it has been "corrupted by the mores of the culture in which it was received."[19]

In summary, the so-called mainstream or reformist feminists are willing to use the Bible—but with drastic selectivity. Those passages supportive of a patriarchal world view (teaching subordination, distinct roles for men and women, etc.) are to be relegated to the marginal areas of the canon, whereas those upholding equality in Christ are to be seen as determinative and binding. Yet even here the final authority is not the biblical witness but the current cultural understanding of equality and wholeness which is informed by the social sciences, particularly psychology and sociology.[20] The Bible is read in the light of this cultural understanding, which is not simply intellectual but also experiential. The fact that the cultural vision of a new humanity is an object not only of our hopes but also of our experience means that in the final analysis the authority for faith is experiential and subjective.

The Language of the Bible

The relevance of this discussion to the debate on the language of faith, and especially the language of the Bible, is very clear. Biblical authority is inextricably tied to how we conceive of the imagery or symbolism of the Bible.

Those who accent the total otherness and inaccessibility of God are inclined to view the Bible as more or less opaque in relation to the Word of God. Opaque in this context means virtually impenetrable to understanding.[21] God is known not by thought but by the blind groping of love.[22] What is given in the Bible are "glimmerings of transcendence" (Carl Rasche) rather than real knowledge of God. It is commonly held that we can say of God only what he is not (*via negativa*). This category embraces not only the main strand of feminist theology but also a great many of those in all theological traditions who have been unduly influenced by either Gnosticism or Neoplatonic mysticism.[23]

Those who affirm God as utterly transcendent but not wholly dissimilar to humanity are inclined to view the Bible as translucent to the Word of God. These are the people who stress the middle way of analogy as opposed to univocity on the one hand and equivocity on the other. We can have an imperfect but nevertheless real knowledge of God. We can know the ways of God by faith in Jesus Christ, but we cannot comprehend his essence. Here we find the centrist tradition of Christian faith—Augustine, Thomas Aquinas, Martin Luther, John Calvin, Karl Barth, and Thomas Torrance, among many others.

Those who stress the congruity and homogeneity between God and humanity are prone to regard the Bible as transparent to the Word of God. While acknowledging that the Bible contains symbolism and metaphor as well as historical first-hand report, they nevertheless contend that the basic affirmations of the Bible concerning God and his self-revelation to humanity can be comprehended by human reason (though not exhaustively) and can therefore be stated univocally. These are the people who prefer to think of the Bible as a verbal revelation from God or as a document of revealed propositions. This general position is forcefully argued today by conservative evangelicals like Carl Henry, Gordon Clark, Ronald Nash, and Roy Clouser.[24] It was anticipated by the medieval scholastic theologian Duns Scotus, who believed that it is possible to have a univocal knowledge of God, since every analogy must have a univocal core.[25]

Rationalistic philosophy (as distinguished from the theological rationalism noted above) aims for a univocal rather than merely symbolic knowledge of God, but it usually relegates the biblical language as well as the language of piety and devotion to the category of myth and poetry. Philosophers as different as Whitehead and Hegel argue that we must not abandon the poetic or mythical language of the Bible, but we must clarify it by translating poetic insight into conceptual truth.

Most feminists, as has been indicated, fall into the first position, namely, seeing the Bible as giving us only intimations of transcendence. Gail Ramshaw-Schmidt describes the scriptural language about God as metaphorical rather than univocal or analogical. "A metaphor," she claims, "says something radically other than what we want it to say."[26] Thus the biblical language is characterized by catachresis—using a word or phrase that does not fit.[27] Because God is radically other than humanity, we can only dimly perceive him; he always escapes and transcends our definitions. This is why "human language cannot properly or adequately describe God." I would argue that human language cannot exhaustively describe God, but it can certainly give an adequate description if it is inspired by the Spirit of God—adequate not for a comprehensive knowledge of metaphysical reality but for life and salvation.[28] Ramshaw-Schmidt draws upon Meister Eckhart, the thirteenth and fourteenth century Rhineland mystic, who stressed the utter incongruity of human language about God.[29]

In radical feminism, the emphasis is on knowing God by intuition and feeling rather than conceptually or propositionally. The language about God is mythical and poetic, and this is all we need in order to realize our potential as bearers of divinity.

Those feminists who link up with process philosophy and theology are willing to use Scripture because it offers provocative lures that lead us into the promise of the future. From Scripture we gain not conceptual knowledge of God but instead a new awareness of self and the world, which enables us to embark or continue on the glorious adventure of life.

In opposition to the agnosticism that mysticism spawns, evangelical theology contends that we can speak about God truly, but not exhaustively, because God first speaks to us and awakens within us a possibility to engage in dialogue with the transcendent. Our words in and of themselves cannot reach God, but our words can be adopted by God as means by which we can bear witness to his saving deeds. Our words can also be received by God when they are offered in the form of prayer. Karl Barth has stated it well:

> By the grace of God we shall truly know God with our views and concepts, and truly speak of God with our words. But we shall not be able to boast about it, as if it is our own success, and we have performed and done it. It is we who have known and spoken, but it will always be God and God alone who will have credit for the veracity of our thinking and speaking.[30]

Evangelical theology in the classical tradition upholds revelational translucency over both mystical ineffability and rational transparency. We can know God—partially and yet truly—when we are known by God in the event of the awakening to faith. Faith signifies not the rational grasping of the truth of revelation but the state of being grasped by this truth. The role of reason is neither to prepare the way for revelation nor to measure its validity but instead to serve revelation as we pursue our vocation to be signs and witnesses of the One who is revealed.

The Return to Theonomy

Whereas many traditional religionists are inclined to heteronomy—locating authority in an external standard or institution (such as creed, church, or magisterium)—feminists locate authority in the self—in conscience, experience, or mystical insight (autonomy). Feminist theology is therefore anchored in the Renaissance and Enlightenment, which celebrated the infinite possibilities of man, rather than in Catholic tradition or the Reformation, which emphasized submission to the authority of either the church or the Bible.

It is my position that we need again to retrieve theonomy in order to overcome the present polarity between liberal and conservative religion. The church at its best, both Catholic and Protestant, has maintained a theonomous understanding of authority—in which the final court of appeal is the living Christ himself—the center and ground of human personhood as well as the head of the church and the primary focus and ultimate author of the Bible. In theonomy the self is not negated as in heteronomy, nor is it given free rein to go its own way, as in autonomy; instead, the self is fulfilled in God by losing itself in the service of God.

Against Tillich, however, who freely makes use of this typology, I insist that locating authority in God, the transcendent ground and goal of the self, also entails submitting to his self-revelation in Jesus Christ, the content of the Bible and the basic message of the church. God is known only as he reveals himself in his Word—revealed, written, and proclaimed. We have the infallible norm for faith and practice not by plumbing the depths of our consciousness, but by seeking the Word of God in Scripture primarily and in church tradition secondarily.

This is not, however, to make of either the Bible or the church heteronomous authorities (as has been the case in much theologizing in the past and present). The Bible is not in and of itself infallible or absolutely normative; yet by virtue of the Spirit of God acting upon its words and also moving within our hearts, the Bible directs us to the One who alone is unconditionally infallible—Jesus Christ, the incarnate Word of God, the Son of the Father, the source and ground of all truth. Similarly, the church is not in and of itself infallible, but it becomes infallible when its words become translucent to the living Word of God who stands over the church as its transcendent head but at the same time works within the church as its immanent guide and teacher.

In the light of the feminist protest against sexism and patriarchalism, I believe that we as orthodox Christians must acknowledge that too often in the past we have confused the patriarchal garb in which divine revelation comes to us with the truth of revelation itself. We have been inclined to absolutize cultural expressions and modes of behavior that belong to a cultural past and not to the dogmatic content of the faith itself. We have been guilty of absolutizing certain directives in the Bible that were intended not as universal divine commands but as specific injunctions pertaining to a particular situation in the church (such as Paul's admonition that women keep silent in the churches).

At the same time, we must resist the prevailing practice in modern theology to separate the divine content from the cultural form and to place it in a new symbolic garb. The divine content of the Bible only comes to us in and through the language of Canaan, and though we can supplement this language, we cannot abandon it. Moreover, this language is not an obstacle to the understanding of God but the catalyst and conduit through which we come to the right understanding.

The biblical witness is normative not simply because it points to revelation but because it participates in this revelation through the action of the Spirit; it thereby becomes a part of the revelation itself. We cannot say that Paul was mistaken in his view of subordination, since this is to denigrate the authority and normativeness of his affirmations. Neither dare we say, as does process theologian Lewis Ford, that the Bible has lost its credibility as a norm for faith because of our "greatly expanded world history, a scientific understanding of nature and man, and a drastically altered social and ethical situation."[31] The norms of theology, in his opinion, must now be "purely philosophical criteria."[32]

In the evangelical view, the Bible derives its authority not from its concurrence with one's self-evident preconceptual experience or with the latest findings in the social and natural sciences. Rather its authority is derived from the self-disclosure of the living God in the history that it records and celebrates. The fact that God really did reveal himself in the person of Jesus Christ, the fact that the Word became flesh and dwelt among us, the fact that Jesus Christ really rose from the dead—this is the ineradicable basis upon which Christian faith stands or falls. The authority for faith, however, has not only a historical but also a pneumatic dimension: it rests partly on the outpouring of the Holy Spirit who brings the church into a renewed appreciation of the facts of sacred or biblical history, who opens the minds of believers to the significance of these facts, not only for biblical times, but also for the times in which we live. We look to the Bible, not because it is an outstanding piece of religious literature, a religious or poetic classic, but because it contains the revelation of God's will and purpose for all humankind. It yields not simply glimmerings of transcendence but the knowledge that is able to instruct us for salvation (2 Tm 3:15). This is a knowledge available only to faith, however, not to natural reason, which can attain a historical knowledge of the biblical revelation but not the redeeming knowledge that gives us the existential significance of this revelation. Feminists are right that we need a new horizon of meaning, but this comes to us when we are brought into a saving relationship with Jesus Christ through the preaching and hearing of the gospel (Rom 10:8-17), not through a comparative analysis of cultures or a phenomeno-logical treatment of religious experience.

Our hope lies neither in making contact with the depths of human consciousness nor in blindly submitting to the dictates of church authorities. Instead it lies in joyfully embracing the gospel of reconciliation and redemption, in gladly responding to the great invitation of our Lord to become his sons and daughters on the basis of the promises recorded in the Bible and reaffirmed by our fathers and mothers in the faith through the ages.

SIX

Parallels with the German Christians

Who Were the German Christians?

Feminists who measure the Bible and all areas of life by the yardstick of their collective experience have in recent history what should be to them an acutely embarrassing precedent. In a significant letter to the Joint Office of Worship of the Presbyterian Church (USA), Harold Nebelsick pointed to some striking parallels between the modern feminist movement and the German Christians, a congeries of groups within the churches in Germany during the later 1920s and 1930s that tried to come to an accommodation with National Socialism.[1] Since then, I have done some in-depth research on this issue and have been in correspondence with Professor Nebelsick. In my opinion, the parallels between the two movements are glaring and beyond dispute.

The "German Christians" is a term that covers a wide variety of organizations within the churches of Germany at the time of the rise of Hitler, but they all had one thing in common: they were intent on bringing the message of faith into alignment with the emerging ideology of National Socialism. Some of the German Christians were very close to the racist and nationalist ideology propagated by such thinkers as Alfred Rosenberg, Wilhelm Hauer, General Erich Ludendorff, and

Ernst Bergmann. These votaries of the extreme right were generally hostile to institutional Christianity, seeking to replace it by a new national church that would be Germanic in its basic thrust. The extremist groups within the German Christians generally welcomed these nationalist and racist cultists as allies in the struggle for a new Germany.

We should keep in mind that some of those identified with the Germanic cult movements did not denigrate Christianity completely but sought to conserve what is abiding and reject what is stultifying. Their aim was to purge Christianity of its Jewish elements and unite it with the folklore of the pre-Christian Teutonic tribes. A few in this so-called Third Confession appealed to the racist philosopher Paul de Lagarde, who believed that "there were certain values in Protestantism and in Christianity worth conserving, but this could be done only by fusing them with the Germanic folkgenius."[2] Rosenberg blamed Paul for corrupting the simple faith of Jesus: "Our Pauline churches are not Christian but consciously or unconsciously a gigantic falsification of the message of Jesus."[3] He was willing to accept parts of the Gospels of Mark and John but not the Jewish gospels of Matthew and Luke or any of the letters of Paul.

For Ernst Bergmann, "the German God is the friend-God, not the Jewish tyrant-God."[4] He presented this as his personal credo: "I believe in the God of the German religion who is at work in nature, in the lofty human spirit, and in the strength of his people. I believe in the helper, Christ, who is struggling for the noble human soul."[5] Such a statement of faith reflects the sentiments of the extremist faction within the German Christians, and men like Bergmann could even be included in "German Christianity" in its broad sense.

On the other hand, there were racist cults that chose to break even these tenuous links with traditional Christian faith, calling for a return to the gods of the pre-Christian barbarian tribes. Among these were the Nordic Faith Fellowship; the Germanic Faith Communion; the Society of Native Religion;

the All-German People's Community; the Germanic Faith Fellowship; the Tannenberg Federation, which sacrificed horses to Thor, the god of thunder; the Thula Society; and the German Faith movement of Wilhelm Jacob Hauer. Some of these were not as violently anti-Christian as others and had no compunction in appealing to Christian scholarship in support of their views.

Wilhelm Hauer, a Sanskrit scholar and professor of comparative religion at Tübingen University, manifested this eclectic spirit, acknowledging his indebtedness to Rudolf Otto and the German mystics. For him, the true God is an "eternal divine force" or "eternal creative power" of which the gods are only symbols. In contrast to those in the Germanic folk movements as well as in the German Christian movement itself, who were both anti-liberal[6] and anti-Judaic, Hauer paid respect to the contribution of German liberal theology to the new religious and racial consciousness. "The Schleiermacher of the *Addresses on Religion*," he said, "attempts to liberate Christianity from its Near Eastern Semitic form and out of the Germanic . . . spirit to give it a new basis. And the liberal theology of the nineteenth century of which he was the founder is, when looked at within and to its depths, nothing else than an attempt to Germanize Christianity."[7] Hauer came to the conviction that the time was ripe for a new structure that would be a vehicle for a purely Germanic religion.

In the writings of Hauer and others in the Germanic folkic movements, one can discern a reemergence of the religion of the Earth Mother. Here, for example, is the litany for the marriage consecration in the Germanic Faith movement:

Mother Earth, who lovingly bears us all,
And Father Heaven, who blesses us
with his light and his changing weather,
and all the good powers that inhabit the air,
they rule over you
till your destiny is fulfilled.[8]

Ernst Bergmann, too, contended that we have to think again of God as bisexual. The traditional belief in a Man-God must now be replaced by the belief in "Mother Nature" and the "Great Mother."[9] Bergmann also asserted that man can redeem himself because the inner core of humanity is God.

Among the bright lights in Germanic tradition who were often eulogized in the Germanic folk movements were Meister Eckhart (who had a significant influence on Rosenberg), Richard Wagner, Jacob Boehme, Fichte, Goethe, and Nietzsche (Hitler's favorite philosopher). The mysticism of these cultic movements was more inner-worldly than Neoplatonic, since it was believed that God is found not in detaching ourselves from materiality and temporality but in immersing ourselves in the world. This is why "blood and soil" became so important in some of these groups and in National Socialism as well.

Much of what has been said of the Germanic folk movements also pertains to a great many German Christians in that they had similar aims: a reborn church that would prepare the way for a resurrected Germany based on the new sacreds of blood, race, and soil. Yet instead of a completely new religion, they sought a purified Christianity, divested of its Semitic and Oriental trappings. Both movements called for a resymbolization of the faith in order to bring Christianity into accord with the spirit of the new Germany.

Among the German Christian groups was the Saxon People's Church, which drew up a confession of Twenty-Eight Theses. Alongside a number of orthodox formulations we find: "God orders the life of man in family, people and State. Therefore in the totality claim of the National Socialist State the Church recognizes the call of God to the family, people and State."[10] The Old Testament, it was held, has been superseded by the New Testament, and the former has value only in leading us to the New. The Theological Faculty at Berlin largely defended the Twenty-Eight Theses of these so-called moderate German Christians.

Reinhardt Krause, a spokesman for another branch of the German Christians, the German People's Church, likewise underlined the integral relation between faith and politics: "For the Church absolutely the same laws of life hold as for the State: service to our people is divine service."[11] "We are striving," he said, "for an undivided German People's Church on the basis of a really racial German Christianity according to the principle: one People, one Reich, one Faith."[12]

More radical were the Six Theses for German Christians drawn up in March, 1934, in which Hitler was applauded not only as political leader but also as the true Messiah of the German people: "For the German People the time is fulfilled in Hitler. For through Hitler, Christ, God the Helper and Redeemer, has become mighty amongst us. Therefore National Socialism is positive Christianity in action."[13]

Among the radical German Christians, who gained ascendancy in the movement, the idea of a Creator God is replaced by a God immanent in the historical process. God is no longer Almighty Creator of the world but the soul of the race. Jesus is upheld as the proclaimer of a lofty morality or as a heroic personality. To Bishop Hossenfelder, one of the leaders of the German Christians, "Christ is an heroic fighter, a helper and conqueror, rather than the mediator between God and man."[14] While the moderate wing of the movement chose to regard Jesus as cosmopolitan, the radicals saw him as Aryan. Salvation was held to rest in the courageous will to action rather than in divine grace.

Most of the German Christians were adamantly opposed to missions to the Jews, though they would not go so far as to withhold either the gospel or charity from them. Jews who become Christians, they said, must be regarded as Jewish Christians, not German Christians. Christians of Jewish descent should have their own congregations. Moreover, no marriage is to be allowed between Jews and Germans, even if the Jews happen to be Christians. The German Christians also sought to apply the so-called Aryan paragraph to the life of the church, meaning that Christians of Jewish descent would be barred from holding offices in the church.

With considerable acumen, Arthur Frey points to the perils of the German-Christian synthesis: "If at first the confession of the Gospel of Jesus Christ is in the center of their Creed with a confession of race, blood, and soil thrown in as an addition, in the course of development the relationship is so altered that the National Socialist aims and interests are brought into the center of German Christian activities."[15]

The German Christian movement in the broad sense (including Christian-oriented people in the folk movements) sought to revise not only the vision of faith but also the language of faith. Already in the 1920s Joachim Niedlich, founder of the League for a German Church, urged that the hymn books and liturgy be purged of all Jewish expressions.[16] He edited a "German Matins" for use in church liturgy, which he hoped might serve as the "building stones in the new and holy shrine of Germanism."

What bothered the German Christians was the biblical scandal of particularity—that God should choose to reveal himself only to a particular people, the Jews, and that he should incarnate himself only at one time and place in history. In order to bring the church into alignment with the new cultural consciousness embodied in the National Socialist revolution, the German Christians downplayed the Jewish background of the faith and stressed both its universal and Germanic character. (The Gnostics also generally denigrated the Old Testament heritage of the church.) An attempt was made to show how faith, in order to be truly vital, must link up with the indigenous ideas and practices of the culture in which it finds itself.[17]

What the revisionist program of the German Christians amounted to was a de-Judaizing of the faith. Instead of speaking of "Israel," they chose to refer to "the people of God." Jesus was no longer King of the Jews but now the flower or prototype of a reborn humanity. Salvation, it was said, comes not from the Jews but from the creative, eternal power at work within all cultures and races, reaching unprecedented heights among the Germanic or Aryan peoples. Churches were urged to rid themselves of Jewish names such as "Zion," and Hebraic expressions like "Hallelujah" and "Amen" were removed from prayers. While in 1834 military force had to be used to convince a Lutheran church in Silesia to adopt the slightly modified Union ritual, a hundred years later Protestant congregations offered little or no resistance to proposals for de-Judaizing the language of faith and liturgy.[18]

The German Christians were not only intent to recast the language connoting a particularistic revelation to the Jewish people; they also tried to bring the New Testament ethic of love and humility into accord with the National Socialist ethic of duty and loyalty. Reich Bishop Mueller, in 1936, offered a revised edition of the Sermon on the Mount. A traditional version of Matthew 5:4 reads: "Blessed are they that mourn: for they shall be comforted" (KJV). The new version is: "Happy is he who bears his suffering like a man; he will find strength never to despair without courage."[19]

Although the moderate wing of the German Christians continued to affirm the Trinity, this doctrine was increasingly challenged by the radicals who saw God not as tripersonal but as suprapersonal—as the soul of the race or *Volk*. Jesus Christ was no longer the Word made flesh but a religious hero. No wonder those Christians opposing a rapprochement with National Socialism accused their opponents of both Arianism and Pelagianism.

It is a sad but incontrovertible fact that many leading theologians within the church went over to the German Christians, among them Emanuel Hirsch, Friedrich Wieneke, and Wilhelm Stapel (all representing the liberal wing of the church). Others closer to traditional faith who lent their support to the German Christians, at least at the beginning, were Paul Althaus, Friedrich Gogarten, Heinrich Bornkamm, Gerhard and Helmut Kittel, and Otto Weber (though the last to his credit publicly repented of his precipitous action). It is easy for us living in another society to judge those who fall under the spell of an ideology alien to Christian faith, but we need to remember that we ourselves are vulnerable to ideologies indigenous to our own culture—democratic egalitarianism, feminism, and laissez-faire liberalism (now called conservatism).

We should also recognize that not all church people succumbed to the beguilements of the German Christians. Among those who adamantly protested against the proposed rapprochement with National Socialism was the eminent Swiss theologian Karl Barth. Barth, who for a time held teaching positions at several German universities, saw "German Christianity" as the sorry culmination of Neo-Protestantism (which began already in the Enlightenment)—the attempt to bring Christian faith into accord with the values and ideals of modern culture. He declared in 1933: "If the Confession of the Church is to be expanded, that must be done according to the standard of Holy Scripture, and in no case according to the standard of any world-view, political or other, prevailing at a particular time."[20] For, he continued, "not by blood and therefore not by race is the fellowship of those who belong to the Church determined, but by the Holy Spirit and Baptism."[21]

Barth was the principal author of the Barmen Declaration, the catalyst for the confessing Church in Germany which drew together Lutherans, Reformed, and free church people in a united opposition to National Socialism and the German Christians. Its attack on natural theology is especially significant for our discussion: "*We reject the false doctrine* that the Church might and must acknowledge as sources of its proclamation, except and beside this one Word of God, still other events, powers, forms and truths as God's revelation."[22] Among the bold spirits who identified themselves with the Confessing Church were Martin Niemoeller, Bishop Hans Meiser, Hans Asmussen, and Dietrich Bonhoeffer.

Voices representing the older Lutheran confessionalism were also raised against the National Socialist ideology. We should especially take note of the Young Reformation movement, which included Walter Künneth, Karl Heim, Hans Lilje, and Wilhelm Stählin. This movement imagined, however, that it could work with the German Christians in counteracting the nationalist and racist religion of Nordic or Aryan paganism.[23] Its efficacy in resisting the new paganism was thereby undermined.

Biblical-Cultural Synthesis in America

The sad history of the German Christian experiment in Germany has obvious parallels in the American situation. The feminist movement is a glaring example, though there are others, which I shall mention in this section.

First, I shall proceed to examine in some detail the parallels between ideological feminism and German Christianity. The most important is that both movements prove to be forms of natural theology. In addition to the revelation of God in Holy Scripture, feminists, like the German Christians, appeal to new revelations in nature and history. What God has said in the past is deemed less important than what God is saying now in the political and social upheavals of our time. Again, both movements sound the call to liberation from political and economic oppression. The German Christians spoke on behalf of the German people, who were struggling to cope with growing unemployment and spiraling inflation stemming in part from the excessive war reparations imposed by the triumphant allied forces. Feminists champion the cause of women who have been and continue to be discriminated against in a largely patriarchal society. Both German Christians and feminists appeal to pre-Christian forms of religion. Just as the former sought to incorporate the religion of the old Teutonic tribes, so Rosemary Ruether and other feminists seek a synthesis of Canaanite goddess religion and biblical prophetic religion. In both cases naturistic mysticism triumphs over biblical monotheism.

Again, German Christians and feminists alike press for a resymbolization of the faith in order to give a fresh expression to the new social vision. Both deemphasize the Old Testament and Paul (here we see a mutual kinship to Gnosticism); the German Christians objected to the Jewish character of both, whereas the feminists object to the patriarchalism they find in both. Each of these movements supports a revision of biblical and liturgical language; one is concerned to depatriarchalize the language of faith and Scripture, the other to de-Judaize it. Finally, in both movements one can discern a pronounced utopian thrust—the illusive expectation that a new social order free of exploitation and oppression is a viable possibility within history.

One might well object that modern feminism is inspired by lofty motivations, by the vision of equality between the sexes and races, whereas the German Christians were motivated by an insular nationalism and racism. Yet it would be doing an injustice to the German Christians to view them in completely negative terms. It should be remembered that the National Socialists appealed not only to the lower-middle class and parts of the middle and upper classes but also to a sizable portion of the working class. Many of those identified with the National Socialists, as well as with the German Christians, were painfully aware of the drift of the country toward a socialist or proletarian revolution; they deplored the inability of the Weimar regime in Germany to bring stability and hope to an ailing populace; they were disturbed by the inability of the churches to fill the spiritual vacuum in the German soul. Hermann Rauschning indicates that his growing opposition to the Weimar regime was based partly on the fact that it "was deliberately and systematically doing everything to promote the secularization of our life and to cut men loose from the transcendental roots of their existence."[24] Feminists, too, are moved to action by the inequities and contradictions, as well as the spiritual hunger, that they see in contemporary society. Unable to cope with the pressures of such a profound sense of malaise, many feminists find their scapegoat in the male chauvinists, just as the German Christians and the Nazis found their scapegoat in the Jews.

Feminism and socialism represent ideologies on the left, but there is also a growing temptation in our country to ally Christianity with rightist ideology (as there was in prewar Germany). According to the late Huey Long, if fascism ever came to America, it would come in the guise of Americanism. (He has also been reported as saying—in the guise of democracy.) At present, the political mood in our nation is slanted toward the right. The myth of Manifest Destiny in which America is seen as the New Israel destined to be a light to the nations is very appealing to religious conservatives, both Protestant and Catholic.[25] The impassioned support of evangelical conservatives for the ideology of Zionism dovetails neatly with the current policy of America's government in siding with Israel over the Palestinians, a policy readily endorsed by both Republicans and Democrats.

While it is true that in general religious conservatives do not wish to rewrite the language of faith and liturgy, they are more and more rewriting the language of history—viewing the signers of the Declaration of Independence as evangelical Christians rather than the deists and agnostics most of them were.[26] The appeal to the American cultural experience with an emphasis on the values of freedom, autonomy, and change, is present in both liberal and conservative theological movements. The celebration of the American heritage as a beacon of hope for all humankind is a further sign of the emergence of a natural theology based on the appeal to a second source of revelation—the American revolutionary experience and the founding documents of the nation: the Declaration of Independence and the Constitution.

Is commitment to the American dream espoused by religious conservatives and liberals alike all that different from commitment to the mythical vision of the Third Reich, which activated the German Christians? When Richard Nixon hailed the American space landing on the moon as the most significant event in world history, he was expressing the same kind of nationalistic or tribalistic sentiment that we witnessed in the German Christians.

What is also noticeable in the religious right are sporadic but growing attempts to resymbolize the language of faith.[27] In the positive thinking cult and the New Thought movement, God is often designated as "the Creative Spirit," "the One Great Source," "The Source of Supply," "Unlimited Possibility," the "Unlimited Pool of Power," "the Mighty I Am Presence," and "the Slumbering Deep within You."[28] Similar nomenclature for God can be detected in the New Age movement with its curious blend of evolutionism, racism, and occultism.[29] In all these movements God is an "unfailing resource" or "Spiritual Presence" rather than "Sovereign Lord." Prayer is reduced to visualization or affirmation and negation, whereas in biblical faith it is seen essentially as heartfelt supplication to a holy and almighty God. What is crucial is not the incarnation of God in the Jesus of history but the principle of the abundant life or the ideal of interior peace or the secret of successful living exemplified in Jesus. Instead of the divine commandment, we are directed to spiritual laws, such as the law of reciprocity or the law of sowing and reaping. The goal in life is no longer the service of the glory of God but the realization of human potential.

The synthesis between Christian faith and American religion and philosophy is patently evident in the electronic church movement, which has a rightist rather than a leftist hue. It is also present in the movement of process theology, which is to the left theologically but often in the center or even the right politically, though some strands are allied with democratic egalitarianism and socialism. Both the electronic church and the process movement have to be understood against their background in American transcendentalism, pragmatism, personalism, and utilitarianism. Just as the German Christians sought to celebrate the cultural heroes of German tradition—Meister Eckhart, Luther, Frederick the Great, Schleiermacher, Goethe, Bismarck—so American Christians, both left and right, hold up our cultural heroes—George Washington, Thomas Jefferson, Ralph Waldo Emerson, Henry David Thoreau, Abraham Lincoln, Walt Whitman, Oliver Wendell Holmes, Jr., Theodore Roosevelt. To this list feminists gladly add the names of Susan B. Anthony, Margaret Sanger, Sojourner Truth, Jane Addams, Lucretia Mott, Elizabeth Cady Stanton, and Margaret Mead. Christian feminists might well include Catherine and Evangeline Booth; Phoebe Palmer; Mother Ann Lee, founder of the Shakers; Frances Willard; Mary Baker Eddy; and Amanda Smith. The extreme left also has its patron saints: Thomas Paine (also admired by the right), Nat Turner, Eugene Debs, Saul Alinsky, Cesar Chavez, Angela Davis, and Anna Louise Strong.

National Socialism as an ideology appealed to both the right and the left, to the privileged as well as to the working classes. Yet its emphasis on recovering German identity made it a conservative rather than a radical revolution. In this respect, the new religious right in our country is closer to the political and social concerns of the National Socialist party and the German Christian movement than the left-wing movements, including feminism. At the same time, the affinities and parallels between ideological feminism and the German faith movements are striking enough to give us cause for grave concern.

In a revealing statement, Hermann Rauschning tells what attracted well-meaning Christians to the banner of National Socialism:

> Shall I give you a catalogue of all the things we wanted to achieve with the aid of Nazism? Tradition instead of radicalism, continuity instead of a rationally worked-out

fresh start. Evolution instead of revolution. A form resulting from growth instead of a manufactured apparatus. Self-government instead of bureaucratism. Decentralization instead of centralization. Variety instead of uniformity. Personal initiative instead of tutelage. The individual instead of the collective. Property instead of dependence on incomes drawn from the state. A Christian basis instead of that of the "enlightenment" of rationalism.[30]

National Socialism could not deliver in any of these areas, and the same can be said for the German Christians. This shows that in correcting social wrongs and in resolving issues that divide our people, we must be very careful not to ally the faith of the church with any cultural ideology, especially one offering a quick panacea to social ills.

Ideology and Theology

The conflict between the Confessing Church and the German Christians as well as the present-day furor over feminist attempts to desex the Bible brings us to the complex relation between ideology and theology. Ever since Karl Marx and Karl Mannheim, theologians and philosophers have been alert to the reality of an ideological taint to human reasoning.[31] Both Marx and Mannheim interpreted ideology as the systematic rationalization of the privileged classes to maintain their power and position in society. Following Reinhold Niebuhr, I see the ideological temptation extending to all social classes.

An ideology might be defined as a view of the whole of reality, especially of social and historical reality, that is noticeably colored by class bias or vested interests. An ideology arises not out of dispassionate reflection on metaphysical themes (as in speculative philosophy) but out of commitment to a vision of society that serves the aspirations of the group or class to which one belongs. Because it is governed by ulterior motives, an ideology "produces a distorted picture of the reality of the world, disguises real abuses and replaces rational arguments by an appeal to emotion."[32] An ideology provides not simply an intellectual understanding, but also existential hope and moral guidance. It can therefore be seen as a secular salvation.[33]

Whereas an ideology is committed to advancing the interests of a particular party or group in society, theology is ideally an attempt to reflect on the meaning of the word of God as attested in Holy Scripture and to call people to obedience to this word, even if it entails the sacrifice of vested interests and economic security. Theology, like ideology, has an existential element, but its call is not to preserve or fulfill one's life in the world but to deny one's needs and aspirations for the service of the kingdom that is not of this world. All theologizing is tainted by ideology to some degree, since none of us, even if regenerated by divine grace, can wholly detach ourselves from the pressures and biases of the society in which we live. Yet it is possible to overcome ideological bias in part in moments of prayerful self-transcendence when we make contact with the God who transcends and judges culture and history (Reinhold Niebuhr).

Among ideologies that have been influential in this century are classical liberalism, welfare liberalism, fascism, feminism, pacifism, and socialism. Patriarchalism, too, is an ideology, one having its roots in virtually all ancient cultures. A religious movement, such as evangelicalism or liberalism, can become an ideology or at least inextricably bound up with an ideology so that it is really voicing the economic and cultural biases of its own constituency rather than giving a clear picture of the word of God, which stands in judgment over all ideologies. The opposite of an ideological religion is a prophetic religion, which calls all classes and groups in society to repentance.

Feminist theologians have been quick to detect the ideological cast of patriarchalism. Sheila Collins regards patriarchalism as "a metaphysical world view, a mind-set, a way of ordering reality."[34] At the heart of patriarchalism is the subject-object split in which humanity is set over against God and vice versa. Rosemary Ruether poignantly discerns the "deformation" of Christianity from a prophetic to an ideological religion: "The Prophets . . . made messianic language a judgment on existing kings and a hope for an alternative social order. But when Christianity became an imperial religion, this kingship language was used to sacralize existing Christian monarchs as expressions of divine kingship and representatives of Christ on earth."[35] With some validity, she claims that the

> key to this ideological deformation is the socioreligious group's movement from powerlessness to power. When the religious spokespersons identify themselves as members of and advocates of the poor, then the critical-prophetic language maintains its cutting edge. When the religious spokespersons see themselves primarily as stabilizing the existing social order and justifying its power structure, then prophetic language becomes deformed in the interests of the status quo.[36]

While feminists have been ready to expose the ideological character of patriarchal thought and practice, they have not been nearly as acute in discerning the ideological basis for revolutionary thought and practice. An exception is Elisabeth Schüssler-Fiörenza who openly—even proudly—acknowledges her ideological commitment:

> Against the so-called objectivity and neutrality of academic theology, feminist theology maintains that theology always serves certain interests and therefore has to reflect and critically evaluate its primary motives and allegiance. Consequently, theology has to abandon its so-called objectivity and has to become partisan. Only when theology is on the side of the outcast and oppressed . . . can it become incarnational and Christian.[37]

When a theology becomes consciously ideological, as in some forms of feminist and liberation theologies, it is bound to lose sight of the transcendent divine criterion, the living Word of God, by which alone it can determine the validity of its social valuations. Its tie to the revolutionary aspirations and hopes of the oppressed becomes itself the criterion by which it judges the voice of tradition as well as the Scriptures. This is why Fiorenza can say: "No biblical text can claim the authority of scripture if it promotes dehumanization and oppression."[38]

As an ideology, feminism is very much alert to the exploitation and oppression of women, but at the same time it is often glaringly insensitive to the legitimate needs and aspirations of some other marginal or minority groups. For example, while committing itself unreservedly to an Equal Rights Amendment, it fails to appreciate that such an amendment could threaten the rights of other groups such as Orthodox Jews, ethnic Catholics, Hutterites, and Amish, all of whom believe that there are definite roles for men and women, especially in the area of church administration and worship, and may therefore maintain single-sex schools. I am not here judging the rightness or wrongness of these positions, but in a pluralistic society such as ours, group that adhere to the patriarchal ethos for religious reasons need to have their rights respected as well.

Ideological commitment and deformation are almost inevitable in all social conflict. This is why political parties much more than churches are susceptible to the spell of ideologies. When Mario Cuomo offered this new commandment in his keynote speech at the Democratic Party convention in San Francisco in July, 1984, "You shall not sin against equality," he was speaking out of an ideological commitment—probably to both feminism and socialism. From the perspective of Christian faith, sin is always directed against God, not against an abstract social principle, such as equality, and while our faith teaches the equality of all sexes, races, and classes in Christ, it does not necessarily lend support to the ideological notion of equality in the sense of affirmative action, which is rooted in the struggle of disinherited peoples for power and privilege.

Those who seek change for the sake of change are almost invariably committed to an ideology bent on social restructuring. Some of us in the Reformed tradition like to cite the motto originating with Gilbertus Voetius, *ecclesia reformata semper reformanda* (the church reformed and always being reformed), in support of innovations in doctrine and liturgy. We should heed this timely warning of Professor Nebelsick:

> The church is *re*formed not *de*formed in response to the Word which is itself formed according to the witness of scripture. The Reformation and the meaning of the motto was not a "search for the new." Exactly the opposite was the case. The new and the innovative, which had characterized the development of the Medieval Church, and which had been introduced without the authority of Scripture were the very things the Reformers of the sixteenth century attempted to purge from the church. For them nonscripturally authorized innovation was a prime mark of heresy. The Reformers changed the church to be sure, but they changed it by returning to its scriptural base, i.e., by *re*forming it. Legitimate changes in the church therefore are those which the Word, as based upon the witness of Scripture, demands. That is what the *semper reformanda* the "being changed" as over against change for the sake of change and innovation according to our own desires and ideologies is all about.[39]

German Christians claimed to discern the hand of God in the political upheavals of post-World War I Germany. In the light of this new wisdom they sought to alter the historical faith, including the language of faith, in order to bring it into accord with the *Zeitgeist*, the spirit of the times. Surely knowledge of this grim precedent should spur us to hone our critical faculties when both liberals (liberationists and feminists) and ideological new rightists in our society look primarily, not to Scripture, but to the new disclosures of God's will and purpose in the contemporary history of our people.

For theology, unlike ideology, holds that truth is not discovered by committing oneself unreservedly either to the revolutionary struggles of our age or to the preservation of the American way of life. Instead, truth has been revealed once for all in the particular history recorded in the Bible, the history that culminates in the self-revelation of God in Jesus Christ. It is from this vantage point, which is not simply historical but transcendental, that we can judge the relative truth and error in movements within history, both religious and sociopolitical, that claim to speak in the name of God or Christ.

SEVEN

The Growing
Church Conflict

Doctrinal Erosion

The inability of the various factions in the church to resolve the dispute on inclusive language for God reveals a growing conflict in the church (*Kirchenkampf*). These tensions run deeper than the controversy over language, for they have to do with the dogmatic as well as the ethical stance of the church in our times. Yet the language issue is inextricably involved in both these aspects of the church's life and mission.

The conflict in the church in our day must be seen against the background of the erosion of the formula associated with Nicene orthodoxy that God is three persons (*hypostases*) in one nature or substance (*ousia*). Although the language was derived from Hellenistic philosophy, the intent was basically faithful to the biblical witness, namely, that God exists within himself as a fellowship of three agencies or foci of consciousness within the overarching unity of one Absolute Subject. The doctrine of the Trinity is a mystery intelligible but not comprehensible to the finite mind (Thomas Aquinas), and yet we can make some sense of it when it is illumined by metaphors drawn from experience, such as ice, water, and steam, or lover, beloved, and love itself (Augustine).

As the church fathers so cogently perceived, the doctrine of the Trinity is intimately bound up with the doctrine of the deity of Jesus Christ. Indeed, it was out of the Christological disputes that the doctrine of the Trinity was formulated. Because Jesus Christ is true God as well as true man, we need to see how his deity is related to the deity of the Father who is distinct from him and yet one with him (cf. Jn 10:29, 30; Heb 1:3).

The heresies that troubled the church in the early period of its history are still with us today—only in new forms. According to modalism, God manifests himself in three different ways or modes but is in himself an absolute unity or simplicity, not a triunity. In Neoplatonic philosophy God is the One beyond all differentiation and temporality, even beyond good and evil. Arianism held that the true God is impassible and unchangeable and that Christ is a created intermediary between this entirely transcendent God and humanity. Christ is less than God but more than man. Many of the mystics, with profound affinities with Neoplatonism, maintained an agnostic attitude concerning our knowledge of the transcendent God, claiming that we cannot know God in himself or God in his essence but only the effects of God in nature and history.[1] At the other extreme was the heresy of tritheism, which depicted the Godhead as three separate beings, whereas orthodoxy affirmed three subsistences within one nature or being.

Feminist theology is only one of several theological movements calling into question the Trinitarian faith of the church. We see this in the work of Marjorie Suchocki, who is both a process theologian and a feminist theologian.[2] She maintains that God should be named the "One," for "it is the single unity of God" which accounts for the living symphony which is the divine life in the world. While acknowledging "the infinite complexity in . . . the divine nature," she says that to use the word *Trinity* to denote this complexity is to extend the word "far beyond its traditional meaning of threeness."[3] In her view, "Father, Son, and Spirit" are "historically relative expressions of God for us," but we should not "push the distortions back into the nature of God."[4] The Trinity can still be useful as a symbol of the "awesome complexity of God," but this complexity refers not to God in himself apart from the world but to God as he encompasses the world as the all-inclusive world spirit.

Other process theologians likewise reveal a significant departure from the Trinitarian faith, though at least some of them continue to use trinitarian symbols. While Lewis Ford speaks of the Trinity, his thought is basically unitarian, not trinitarian.[5] He envisions a unipersonal God who interacts with the world on the basis of his own dipolarity of nature. As with Whitehead, God is not a triadic self-communication; instead, the dynamism in this God is "the dyadic interrelationship of actuality and possibility."[6]

In Karl Rahner we see an emergent subordinationism.[7] The Word and Spirit appear to be two arms of the one God held out to the world by the Father. Only the Father is God in himself (*autotheos* in Origen's sense). The Son and the Spirit are merely personified extensions of his divinity. Rahner refuses to speak of three persons but instead refers to "three distinct modes of subsisting." By asserting that the economic Trinity is the immanent Trinity, he does not have a Trinity that exists before and apart from the world but one that is always involved in the world process (à la Hegel).

Similarly for Moltmann, the Trinity signifies the unfolding of God in the processes of nature and history. There is no supernatural Trinity but only the self-realization of divinity in world history. God is no longer "an absolutist sovereign in heaven" but a passionate God, the one "who suffers by virtue of his passion for people."[8] Creation is conceived as light breaking forth from God and light "flooding back into God." Human history is interpreted as "God's deliverance from the sufferings of his love" as it seeks fulfillment "in the love that is bliss."[9] Classical Reformed theology, on the other hand, interprets history in the light of God's deliverance of his people from the pains of hell which they deserve to suffer because of sin against his holy law. In the manner of Hegel, he says that we should not think of "God in history" but of "history in God."[10] God is not a "person projected in heaven" but the creative unfolding of the Eternal Spirit in history. Therefore we do not pray *to* God but *in* God, in the event of creative love.

Pannenberg, who is also indebted to Hegel, likewise rejects the God of classical theism, the God who is a transcendent "self-contained being" before and apart from other beings.[11] God is instead "the power of the future" whose deity will be revealed in the consummation of the historical process. Pannenberg dismisses the idea of Jesus as "the *Logos* of God in the sense of a distinct hypostasis existing alongside the Father."[12] The Trinity is to be understood in terms of God's emptying himself into the other, which explains both his own life and the life of the world. For Pannenberg, it seems, the doctrine of the Trinity arises out of the dialectic within history between God the Father and his Word of regeneration; the Spirit simply becomes the depth dimension of the Word. No wonder that one of his critics contends that Pannenberg basically has "a dyadic concept of God" which predominates "over a triadic or trinitarian one."[13]

For Paul Tillich, whose theology is a welcome resource for modern Christian feminists, we should think of the Trinity as "moments within the process of the divine life" as it is realized in the world.[14] The Trinity is a symbol not of God in himself but of the intricacies of the divine-human relationship. The distinctions that come to the fore concerning God pertain not to the Godhead itself but to "the dynamics of human conscious being as it seeks union with its ground."[15] The true God is the "God above God," the undifferentiated unity beyond temporality and multiplicity that nonetheless is the creative source of the world process.

The Dutch Catholic theologian Schoonenberg holds that God becomes a Trinity, something that occurs only in his involvement in history.[16] While he agrees that there is an eternal triadic structure in God himself, this does not take on personal form except in relationship to God's activity in history. Here again we see an attempt to get away from the understanding of Christian supernaturalism that God exists as a fellowship within himself apart from and prior to human history.

While modern theology on the whole wishes to retain the Trinitarian symbolism, it generally understands "Father, Son, and Spirit" as symbols in the sense of metaphors expressing the inexpressible and infinite complexity in God, the infinite depth as well as the creative ground and source of all existence. John Macquarrie says "person" is inappropriate when used nonsymbolically because it then connotes separateness and "inevitable privacy and impenetrability."[17] If the word is used, "the wisest course is to leave the meaning shadowy."[18] William Hill gives this able retort: "But ... there is lacking the option of allowing an analogical power to the use of the term, with the result that its rich potential is left unexplored."[19]

In avant-garde theology, the concept of the Trinity is rooted not in God's self-revelation in Christ but in the experience of the faithful as they seek to understand themselves in relation to the divine presence that they encounter in the world. Susan Thistlethwaite says: "The concept of the Trinity is an attempt to explain the experience believers have had of God's activity in the world."[20] The basis then of the doctrine of the Trinity is both cultural and religious experience rather than God's witness to himself in Holy Scripture.

The erosion of the traditional doctrine of the Trinity stems partly from a misguided apologetic attempt to make the faith credible or palatable to the modern mind. Joseph Bracken's remarks are typical:

If belief in the Trinity is to be genuinely relevant to our present generation, it must be interpreted in terms appropriate to contemporary self-understanding. That is, human beings are more aware than ever before of the need for community, of the fact of change or development, often accompanied by deep suffering, in human life, and finally of the distinctively bisexual character of all human relations. If the concept of God, specifically of God as triune, does not in some way reflect these all-pervasive human concerns, then it will cease to be truly relevant to present-day men and women.[21]

One can only hope that God is as acutely aware as the author of his need for relevance and will conduct himself accordingly!

With the eclipse of the classical understanding of the Trinity as formulated at Nicaea and reaffirmed by Augustine and the mainstream of Catholic, Orthodox, and Protestant theology, we naturally witness a correlative demise of the classical doctrine of Christ (as affirmed at Chalcedon). Jesus Christ is no longer the preexistent Word made flesh but now the symbol of transformed human identity (Tillich) or of the perfect man of God whose consciousness of God's will for him determines his divinity (Moltmann). Sallie McFague confidently decrees: "While we look through the story of Jesus to gain an understanding of what it means to live under God's rule, we cannot make the illegitimate move of identifying Jesus with God."[22] For McFague the incarnation is a symbol that must not be identified with that to which it points. Metaphors, she reminds us, point not to objects but to relationships.

According to Rosemary Ruether, Jesus of Nazareth can be regarded as "a positive model of redemptive humanity. But this model must be seen as partial and fragmentary, disclosing from the perspective of one person, circumscribed in time, culture, and gender, something of the fullness we seek. We need other clues and models as well, models drawn from women's experience, from many times and cultures."[23] For Ruether, Christ is not to be "encapsulated ... in the historical Jesus."[24] We can encounter Christ now in the form of our sister as well as of our brother. God becomes for Ruether "that great collective personhood ... in which our achievements and failures are gathered up, assimilated into the fabric of being, and carried forward into new possibilities."[25]

It seems that in the new theology Jesus is the clue to the divinity within all of us, a divinity we can realize through vicarious identification with the trials and sufferings of the oppressed. What we see in Jesus is not the incarnation of God in human flesh at a particular time and place in history but the perfect realization of God-consciousness present in all humanity. Jesus is the symbol of divine-human unity, a symbol whose efficacy does not absolutely depend on its historical actualization (Tillich). Because Jesus is treated as a symbol (Tillich) or parable (McFague), what is important is the ideal of authentic selfhood that he reflects, an ideal within the grasp of all people. This ideal, moreover, is manifest not only in the picture of Jesus of Nazareth presented in the Bible, but in other pictures of transformed personalities, women as well as men. John Macquarrie acknowledges Buddha and Confucius (in addition to Jesus) as revelations of "authentic humanity."[26]

Religious and Philosophical Language

The crux of the problem is whether the original language of faith, the biblical language of Canaan, is simply to be seen as the product of a patriarchal and monarchical culture, or whether it is to be received as the God-selected language that is determinative for the meaning of divine revelation itself. I here heartily concur with Thomas Torrance: "What is at stake here is the question whether biblical statements about God—for example, about his Fatherhood in respect to Jesus Christ his incarnate Son—are related to what they claim to signify merely in a conventional way ... or in a real way."[27]

Is the original language of faith to be understood only in terms of cultural and historical factors (*Sitz im Leben*)? Or does it not also have a culture-transcendent dimension by virtue of the revelation it attests and also the inspiration of the Spirit who guided the prophets and apostles in their perceptions as well as in their recording (cf. 2 Pt 1:20, 21; Heb 1:1; 2 Tm 3:16; Rv 1:1-3)?

Here again we must ask: Does the language about God in the Bible give us real information concerning who God is and what his plan and purpose are for the world? Or is it simply a valiant but ultimately self-defeating attempt on the part of the biblical prophets and apostles to describe experiences too deep and overpowering for adequate conceptualization? Does the Bible basically give us only seminal insights into the meaning of life that have a universal significance, or does it give us a true and reliable account of God's actual dealings with a particular people and of a real incarnation of God into human flesh?

Because philosophers generally relegate the Bible to the level of poetry and myth, they contend that the symbols of the Bible need to be translated into concepts that will clarify the original meaning. Henry Nelson Wieman says the concept gives the meaning of the symbol.[28] But is not the meaning of the concept governed by the prior meaning of the symbol? Paul Ricoeur readily acknowledges that though the symbol gives rise to thought, thought must always return to and be informed by the symbol.[29]

The question is whether philosophical concepts become the criterion by which we interpret the symbols of divine revelation or whether they simply serve in the explication of the meaning of these symbols. Joseph Haroutunian makes a telling point that when philosophical concepts are brought into the service of faith, their meaning is transformed by the symbols of revelation.[30] Whereas originally their meaning was literal, it now becomes metaphorical under the impact of revelation. The word "God" as used in philosophy always refers to something that is definite or concrete in terms of human experience—being, process, goodness, substance, or power. When the concept of deity is employed in theology, on the other hand, it becomes severed from its philosophical roots and placed in the context of faith seeking understanding. The God of faith cannot be subsumed under any genus, whether this be process, being, reality, or personality, but all general categories become transformed when subsumed under the God of revelation. We come to know what true being and also true personhood are by God's act of disclosing himself as the living Spirit who eternally is and who eternally becomes (Ex 3:14, 15).

In an effort to counter the position of process theology, which seeks to understand God in terms of the category of process, Haroutunian makes this able rejoinder: God's act of reconciliation in Christ

> is a process not in the world but one that reveals the world as the object of reconciliation. There are processes of moving, living, and thinking in our world. But the process of our reconciliation with God is not analogous to any of these. We do not know this process as we know the others. We know this process by "faith," by finding ourselves in a new relation to all processes. It is a process which transforms the meanings of all other processes such as living, eating, working, and loving.[31]

Haroutunian reminds us that a philosophical framework consists of organizing concepts by which we seek to interpret all of reality. But if these concepts become metaphors through the act of being baptized into the Christian faith, they can no longer fulfill their function as organizing concepts. They are themselves subordinated to a higher criterion of meaning, the criterion given in God's self-revelation in Jesus Christ and reflected and attested in the Bible.

The church fathers freely made use of philosophical terms in delineating the doctrines of the triune nature of God and the two natures of Christ. Concepts like *hypostasis* (subsistence) and *ousia* (substance) played a pivotal role in clarifying the mysteries of the Trinity and the incarnation. What we find in the early creeds, however, was not so much a Hellenization of the faith as a transformation of Hellenistic concepts in the light of the faith. This is not to deny that Hellenizing influences were at work, but for the most part they were countered by a strong commitment to the biblical vision.

Thomas Torrance argues with some cogency that the insight that impressed itself upon the Nicene fathers, namely, that Jesus Christ the incarnate Son is "of one and the same being with God the Father" (the *homoousion*) was not a philosophical construction that intruded into the domain of faith but a conceptual symbol that was laid hold of by faith in the service of the gospel.

> The *homoousion* . . . is not a speculative construction, an attempt to break through to the reality of God by the power of human thought, or an interpretation extrinsically imposed upon the evangelical tradition by the theologians of the church. Rather is it a truth which forced itself upon the understanding of the church as it allowed the biblical witness to imprint its own conceptual pattern upon its mind.[32]

Dietrich Bonhoeffer has these trenchant words on the Chalcedonian Definition, which is often regarded as the basis of scholastic theology:

> Its peculiar character lies in the way in which it cancels itself out. In other words, it shows the limitations of the concepts it employs simply by using them. It speaks of "natures," but it expresses the facts in a way which demonstrates the concept of "natures" to be an inappropriate one. It works with concepts which it declares to be heretical formulas unless they are used paradoxically and in contradiction. It brings the concept of substance which underlies the relationship of the natures to a climax and does away with it. From now on it will no longer be permissible to say

anything about the *substance* of Jesus Christ. Speculation about "natures" is at an end; the notion of substance is superseded. If a development of the Chalcedonian Definition were conceivable, it could not be a development in thought about the relationship of the natures; it would be something else which has still to be mentioned. The Chalcedonian Definition is an objective, but living, statement which bursts through all thought-forms.[33]

Luther, like Aquinas, Calvin, Barth, and many other renowned theologians in the church, was not averse to using philosophical terminology in explaining or clarifying the mysteries of faith, even though he constantly warned against the perils of a biblical-classical synthesis. When Luther said that Christ is "substantially present" in the Lord's Supper, he was taking a philosophical concept and pouring new meaning into it. His intention was that Christ is personally present in the whole Eucharistic action culminating in the eating and drinking of the sacramental bread and wine. "Substance" for him was a dynamic term meaning *ens in actu* ("being in action"), and it cannot be used to support either consubstantiation or impanation, which are rational explanations of what transpires in the Lord's Supper.[34]

I have no objection to making use of philosophical terms or concepts in explicating and delineating the content of the biblical revelation. How can we do otherwise? Yet these terms must always be interpreted in the light of the acts of God in the sacred history mirrored in the Bible; they should not be used to impose on these acts a meaning foreign to the Bible. Such terms as "ground of being," "creative source," "creative process," "all-determining reality," "the unconditional," and "Spiritual Presence" can be helpful in calling attention to dimensions of God's activity in his relationship to the world, but they must be seen as further, rather than nearer, to the original meaning than the more realistic, anthropomorphic, and mainly masculine imagery of the Bible. We cannot pray to the ground of being or to the all-determining reality as such. Nor can we enter into a personal relationship with a God who goes under such names exclusively or primarily. We can meditate on such a God, and it is well to remember that philosophical prayer consists mainly in meditation, reflection, and resignation to the Eternal Spirit that upholds or activates the world rather than in heartfelt supplication to a heavenly Father who really hears and answers the prayers of his people.

Not every philosophical concept lends itself for use in Christian theology. Some concepts, especially those connoting a wholly immanent God, have to be excluded from the language of faith or used only with care and on rare occasions. I am thinking of such symbols for God as "the Womb of Being," "Primordial Matrix," and "World Soul," which militate against the biblical vision of God as Almighty Creator and Lord of the universe.

On the other hand, I think it is possible to describe God as the ultimate ground and depth of all being, so long as we go on to affirm that he is much more than this: he is also the creative source of all being. He is not simply the power of being (Tillich) but the act of being (*actus purus*) that is prior to all being. He is not just the first cause of the universe but the ruler of the universe, the Almighty One who holds the whole world in his hands. He is not so much the spirit of love as the One who loves—unconditionally and spontaneously. He is not only a Supreme Intelligence but also dynamic will and energy. He is not the idea of the Good but the Commander of the Good. He is not simply the highest reality or reality in itself but God in action—creating and remolding reality.

God reveals himself not as the impassible Absolute but as the mighty "I am who I am" (Ex 3:14 NIV) or "I will be who I will be."[35] He is being in act rather than either static being or sheer becoming. He is not the One beyond temporality and materiality but the One who enters into time and history, who calls the worlds into being. He is not a God beyond personality (Tillich, Wieman, McFague) but a living Absolute Subject who is the supremely personal and also the ground and center of human personhood.[36]

This is a God, moreover, who reveals himself as Father, Son, and Holy Spirit. These terms are not simply symbols that point to an undifferentiated unity but names that represent who God really is. According to Suchocki, these designations can only be used equivocally and therefore cannot be determinative for our understanding of God. On the contrary, I hold that these names are to be understood analogously. They signify preeminently what our human notions of fatherhood, sonship, and personhood only imperfectly describe. This is why Barth could say, "God has real hands, not claws like we." He is the preeminent person; our personhood is derivative from and relative to his. It is in the light of his personhood that we come to understand what it means to be a person.

Emil Brunner finds the basis of the doctrine of the Trinity in the biblical testimony itself:

> We are not concerned with the God of thought, but with the God who makes His Name known. But He makes His Name known as the Name of the Father; He makes this Name of the Father known through the Son; and He makes the Son known as the Son of the Father, and the Father as Father of the Son through the Holy Spirit. These three names constitute the actual content of the New Testament message.[37]

The three names, of course, carry no hint of autonomy. In the biblical understanding, Brunner continues, we do not have the Son alongside the Father or the Spirit alongside the Son, which would be tantamount to tritheism. On the contrary, only through the Son do we have the Father; only through the Son do we have the Spirit; and only through the Spirit do we have the Son.[38] The Bible is concerned not with the timeless idea of a universal Fatherhood but with the living and concrete Father of our Lord Jesus Christ.[39]

Brunner's position on the Trinity is not irreproachable, since he sees it mainly as a defensive doctrine to safeguard the content of the New Testament message that God was in Christ reconciling the world to himself (2 Cor 5:19). I prefer to follow Barth in regarding the Trinity as an immediate implication of the fact, form, and content of the biblical revelation.

Meaning is ultimately based on personal relationship rather than on the relationship of subject to object.[40] The Trinity can therefore be best understood not as an object, but as an Absolute Subject who encompasses personal relationship within himself. The mystery of the Trinity is therefore open only to the knowledge of personal acquaintance and not to a purely rational or controlling knowledge. We can know God as Father only when God addresses himself to us as Father and calls us to be his sons and daughters. We can know Jesus Christ as the very Son of God only when the Holy Spirit opens our inward eyes to the meaning of what God has done for us in the life, death, and resurrection of Jesus Christ. We can know Jesus Christ as Lord and Savior only when his Spirit moves us to confess him as Lord and Savior. Then we will come to recognize the bankruptcy of the theology that describes Jesus only as the model of transformative love who "simply aids us in understanding."[41] Jesus is not merely a model of love but the God who loves—even to the point of death on the cross. He does not simply aid us in understanding, but he gives us a new understanding, a new vision of the world seen in the perspective of faith.

The meaning of who God is and of what God has done for us in Christ is not immediately accessible to us, even in the Bible. It is not obvious to those whose spiritual sensibilities have not been awakened by grace. On our own we can come to a historical knowledge of the realities that faith describes but not to an existential or redemptive knowledge.

God does not reveal his glorious presence to us directly, for otherwise we would be overwhelmed by the splendor of his majesty. He condescends to meet us in the earthen vessel of the biblical and prophetic testimony. Our inability to fathom the mystery of the truth of God lies not only in our sin and finiteness but also in the manner in which God reveals himself.

The light of God's truth is refracted through the Bible more than being resplendent in the Bible. It is partially veiled in the language and thought world of the Bible even while it is being revealed. We can know—but by faith only, not by sight (1 Cor 2:9, 10; 2 Cor 5:7). Our knowledge of the truth of God is analogical, not univocal. It is adequate for a right understanding but not for a comprehensive or full understanding. It is also adequate and indeed crucial for our salvation.

Although our knowledge of God is analogical and not univocal, it has a univocal reference—God's witness to himself in the saving events testified to in Holy Scripture. Our knowledge of God is analogical, but God's knowledge of us is univocal.[42] Because the word of God—the overarching criterion of meaning—always remains the word of *God,* this criterion is the literal ground and goal for our analogical statements about God. We can experience this word, but we cannot grasp it in our experience.[43] We can perceive this word through the power of the Spirit, but only brokenly and dimly.[44] As soon as we try to reflect on it and conceptualize it, we are already thinking analogically. This light from above, the living word of God, is the metaphysical criterion that overturns our concepts and reshapes and purifies our language. In the moment of decision, our thought patterns are turned in an altogether new direction—toward a reality we can believe in but never possess.

If God were only the highest idea or an absolute or deified object, then there would be no insurmountable problem in coming to a universally agreed understanding of his nature and attributes. An idea is within the purview of human reason, and so there is at least the possibility that human beings can arrive at such knowledge.[45] On the other hand, because God is an Absolute Subject, a living person, in a trinity of interrelations, he can be known only as he makes himself known. We can know him only when he speaks his Word and when we hear in faith. It is the contention of evangelical theology that God has spoken his Word decisively and definitively in the person of Jesus Christ, and the original witnesses to this self-revelation of God in Christ are the prophets and apostles of Holy Scripture. Because God has spoken once for all times (*Einmaligkeit*) in Jesus Christ (Heb 7:27; 9:26), it is mistaken and fallacious to look for a new revelation that will supersede or complement the revelation recorded in the Bible. To know God we must search the Scriptures confidently hoping and expecting that the Spirit will guide us into all truth (Jn 16:13) if we look in faith to Jesus Christ.

The language of the Bible is for the most part symbolic (metaphorical and analogical), though it also includes concepts and conceptual metaphors. The pivotal question is: Do the biblical symbols describe inner experiences projected on the plane of history (Bultmann), or do not they purport to describe real events—what God has actually done in history? Not everything that the Bible reports is to be taken literally, but where the author clearly intends to portray a literal happening, then we are bound to this interpretation. It is not only the event of revelation but the prophetic and apostolic interpretation of this event (which is in part determined by the impact of the revelatory event) that is normative for the understanding of faith.

When Jesus said, "This is my body," the meaning he intended to convey was that he would be personally present to the people of faith in and with this sacramental bread and wine. The words denote a synecdoche, a figure of speech representing the greater or whole thing with only a part.[46] Yet the reality they point to is not something ephemeral or mystical, such as an inward experience of a spiritual presence, but something literal or actual—a real communion with the living Christ given in, with, and under the bread and wine as they are received in faith.

Similarly, when the apostle confesses that Jesus was the Word made flesh (Jn 1:14; cf. Rom 1:3; 2 Cor 5:21; Gal 4:4; Heb 2:14; 1 Tm 3:16), he is referring not to an experience of the divine presence within earthly reality but to a definite act of God whereby God entered history at a particular time and place in the form of a particular man—Jesus of Nazareth. When that same apostle reports the words of Jesus that he is one with the Father (Jn 10:30), this should be taken to mean not a oneness in will only (which is a possibility for all people) but a unity in being, even though there is a distinction within this unity.

The symbols of faith cannot, of course, be fully or truly understood when taken by themselves. They must all be seen in the light of God's act of reconciliation and redemption in Jesus Christ, the overarching symbol that gives meaning and continuity to the myriad of symbols in Scripture. It is not just the symbol of God's redemptive action in Christ but the act itself that is to be viewed as the transcendental criterion of meaning in biblical faith. It is not simply how the prophets or apostles described this event or series of events but how the Holy Spirit interprets these events to the prophets and apostles and to us today. The revelation of God in Christ attested in Scripture is self-authenticating insofar as the Spirit validates and confirms to our hearts what he guided the prophets and apostles to describe and report. Our task is to receive this, to celebrate this, and to witness to this in our words as well as in our deeds.

In this time of a growing church conflict over language about God, it is imperative that evangelical Christians take an uncompromising stand against immanentalism and naturalism, which are the principal threats to the faith today. Just as the people of Israel had to maintain the purity of the faith in the battle against the cult of the Mother Goddess and just as the early Christians had to resist the lure of Gnostic attempts to dilute the particularistic claims of the faith, so Christians today have to contend for the religion of Christ crucified and risen in the face of the unnerving recrudescence of both Baalism and Gnosticism.

Yet though there is a necessary place for polemics in the theological task, we must never lose sight of the fact that our principal calling is to confess what God has done for us and for the whole world in Jesus Christ. Even while we have to utter a resounding *no* to heterodoxy and heresy, we must unite in a still more powerful *yes* to God's gracious election and redemption of the whole world in Jesus Christ. Our proclamation must be undergirded and fulfilled in polemics and apologetics, but it must always be informed by a personal encounter and communion with the living God himself who meets us through the power of his Spirit in the person and work of his only begotten Son, Jesus Christ.

Notes

Chapter One
The Current Debate

1. For a brilliant defense of traditional and mostly patriarchal values in face of women's liberation, see George F. Gilder, *Sexual Suicide* (New York: Bantam Books, 1975).
2. See *Guidelines for Inclusive Language* (New York: United Church of Christ, 1983), p. 6.
3. See *Eternity*, vol. 35, no. 7 (July-August 1984), p. 11.
4. *The Christian Century*, vol. 101, no. 18 (1984): 545.
5. Sandra Dillard-Rosen, "Using 'Goddesses' Can Be Woman's Life-Shaping Choice," *Denver Post*, April 12, 1984, pp. 1B, 2B.
6. Elizabeth Achtemeier, "The Translator's Dilemma: Inclusive Language," *Interpretation*, vol. 38, no. 1 (January 1984), p. 66.
7. Peter McGrath and David Gates, "Scrubbing the Scriptures," *Newsweek*, October 24, 1983, p. 112.
8. Richard N. Ostling, "O God Our [Mother and] Father," *Time*, October 24, 1983, p. 57.
9. Gail Ramshaw-Schmidt, "Lutheran Liturgical Prayer and God as Mother," *Worship* 52 (1978): 529.
10. For a trenchant critique of ideological feminism, see Juli Loesch, "Weaknesses of Feminist Theology," *New Oxford Review* vol. 51, no. 10 (December, 1984), pp. 8-12.
11. Jurgen Moltmann, *The Trinity and the Kingdom*, trans. Margaret Kohl (San Francisco: Harper & Row, 1981), p. 127.
12. See James Luther Adams, *Paul Tillich's Philosophy of Culture, Science, and Religion* (New York: Harper & Row, 1965), pp. 92-94.
13. Paul Tillich, *Systematic Theology*, 3 vols. (Chicago: University of Chicago Press, 1951-63), 3:293-94.
14. Ibid., 1:252.
15. Charles Hartshorne, *Omnipotence and Other Theological Mistakes* (Albany, N.Y.: State University of New York Press, 1984), p. 58.
16. Ibid.
17. Ibid., p. 32.
18. Among feminists who seek to utilize the insights of process philosophy and theology are Mary Daly, Carter Heyward, Denise Larder Carmody, Marjorie Hewitt Suchocki, Patricia Wilson-Kastner, Rosemary Ruether, and Susan Brooks Thistlethwaite.

19. Gnosticism represented a syncretistic religion in the Middle East that antedated Christianity but assumed Christian forms. Its distinctive note was its claim to a special or esoteric knowledge (*gnosis*) that was available only to the pneumatics or spiritual ones. While Platonism and Neoplatonism saw the light of God reflected in the creation, Gnosticism regarded the created or phenomenal world as evil. The two great Christian Gnostics were Valentinus and Basilides.

20. Kurt Rudolph, *Gnosis: The Nature and History of Gnosticism*, trans. P.W. Coxon, K.H. Kuhn, and R.M. Wilson, ed. Robert McLachlan Wilson (San Francisco: Harper & Row, 1983), p. 80.

21. Elaine Pagels, *The Gnostic Gospels* (New York: Random House, 1979), p. 58.

22. Feminists who seem open to or have been influenced by Gnostic spirituality include Mary Daly, John Dart, Matthew Fox, Margot Adler, Rebecca Oxford-Carpenter, Elaine Pagels, Mary E. Giles, Pheme Perkins, and Rosemary Ruether. Ruether appreciates the Gnostic affirmations of the bisexuality of God and the essential equality of man and woman. She takes issue, however, with the Gnostic denigration of bodily existence. She also raises the question whether Gnosticism really overcame the androcentric principle. See Rosemary Ruether, *Sexism and God-Talk* (Boston: Beacon Press, 1983), pp. 36, 37, 100, 101.

The Gnostic character of Mary Daly's theology is clarified by Ruether: "Daly's vision moves to a remarkable duplication of ancient Gnostic patterns, but now built on the dualism of a transcendent spirit world of femaleness over against the deceitful anticosmos of masculinity." Ruether, *Sexism and God-Talk*, p. 230. Daly refers to herself as a "Nag-Gnostic." See Mary Daly, *Pure Lust: Elemental Feminist Philosophy* (Boston: Beacon Press, 1984).

23. Rudolph, *Gnosis*, p. 257.

24. See Stephan A. Hoeller, *The Gnostic Jung and the Seven Sermons to the Dead* (Wheaton: Theosophical Publishing House, 1982).

25. See Geddes MacGregor, *Gnosis* (Wheaton: Theosophical Publishing House, 1979). For a devastating critique of Gnosticism from a biblical perspective see Hans Jonas, *The Gnostic Religion* (Boston: Beacon Press, 1963). Jonas shows the Gnostic roots of modern existentialism and nihilism.

Chapter Two
The Enigma of God-Language

1. See Thomas Aquinas, "The Names of God," in Anton C. Pegis, ed., *Basic Writings of Saint Thomas Aquinas* (New York: Random House, 1945), vol. I, pp. 112-34.

2. One could say that while univocal predication is exact or direct, and equivocal predication is uncertain, analogical predication is approximate but not deceptive. For further reading on this subject see James F. Anderson, *The Bond of Being: An Essay on Analogy and Existence* (St.

Louis: B. Herder Book Co., 1949); and George P. Klubertanz, *St. Thomas Aquinas on Analogy* (Chicago: Loyola University Press, 1960).

3. Tillich, *Systematic Theology*, 2: 9-10.

4. See Paul Ricoeur, *Interpretation Theory: Discourse and the Surplus of Meaning* (Fort Worth: Texas Christian University Press, 1976); "Biblical Hermeneutics," *Semeia* 4 (1975): 75-106; *The Symbolism of Evil*. Trans. Emerson Buchanan (N.Y.: Harper & Row, 1967); *The Rule of Metaphor* (Toronto: University of Toronto Press, 1977); Charles E. Reagan and David Stewart, eds., *The Philosophy of Paul Ricoeur: An Anthology of His Work* (Boston: Beacon Press, 1978); and Lewis S. Mudge, ed., *Essays on Biblical Interpretation* (Philadelphia: Fortress, 1980).

5. Sallie McFague, *Metaphorical Theology* (Philadelphia: Fortress Press, 1982).

6. Ibid., p. 17.

7. F.W. Dillistone, *Christianity and Symbolism* (London: Collins, 1955), p. 161.

8. McFague, *Metaphorical Theology*, p. 17.

9. Thomas F. Torrance, *Reality and Evangelical Theology* (Philadelphia: Westminster Press, 1982), p. 27.

10. McFague, *Metaphorical Theology*, p. 117.

11. Pannenberg prefers the term "paronymy" to "analogy" as Thomists understand this. According to George Kehm, "Paronymous words are words derived from the same root which are related to each other as the substantive, adjective, verb, etc. formed from that root, e.g., just, justly, justice. It cannot be assumed, however, that there is a precisely corresponding meaning between these forms." In Wolfhart Pannenberg, *Basic Questions in Theology*, trans. George H. Kehm (Philadelphia: Westminster Press, 1983), 1: 213.

12. Pannenberg, *Basic Questions in Theology*, 1: 219.

13. Ibid.

14. Ibid., p. 214.

15. Ibid., pp. 237, 238.

16. Ibid., p. 233.

17. Kenneth Hamilton, *Words and the Word* (Grand Rapids: Eerdmans, 1971), p. 106.

18. Avery Dulles, *Models of Revelation* (New York: Doubleday & Co., 1983), p. 133.

19. Ibid., p. 132.

20. Ibid., p. 280.

21. Ibid., p. 257.

22. Ibid., p. 281.

23. Ibid., p. 283.

24. I contend that analogues are nevertheless symbolic, since their meaning-content is not directly apprehensible but can only be inferred. This is made abundantly clear in the contemporary discussion on whether God should be called *Father* or *Lord*. For feminists these terms have come to

have a univocal meaning in this context and therefore must be abandoned.

Although making a distinction between analogy and symbol, Macquarrie often uses the words interchangeably. He argues that because there must be some likeness between a symbol and what it signifies, a symbol basically partakes of the analogical. See John Macquarrie, *God-Talk* (New York: Harper & Row, 1967), pp. 215-30.

25. Maloney cites Gregory of Nyssa with approbation: "Concepts create idols and only wonder lays hold upon something." George A. Maloney, *Pilgrimage of the Heart* (San Francisco: Harper, 1983), p. 13. For Maloney our knowledge of God is existential rather than conceptual. See also Maloney, *A Theology of "Uncreated Energies"* (Milwaukee: Marquette University Press, 1978), pp. 54-59.
26. Gordon Kaufman, *God the Problem* (Cambridge, Mass.: Harvard University Press, 1972), p. 113.
27. Gail Ramshaw-Schmidt, lecture at the Twin Cities Presbytery meeting, Hope Presbyterian Church, Richfield, Minn., May 8, 1984.
28. Virginia Ramey Mollenkott, *The Divine Feminine* (New York: Crossroad, 1983), p. 37.
29. Thomas F. Torrance, *The Ground and Grammar of Theology* (Charlottesville: University Press of Virginia, 1980), p. 167.
30. Thomas F. Torrance, *Transformation and Convergence in the Frame of Knowledge* (Grand Rapids: Eerdmans, 1984), p. 317.
31. Ibid.
32. Hamilton, *Words and the Word*, p. 68.
33. Paul Tillich gives an insightful analysis of how words derived from Hellenistic culture are transformed under the impact of the biblical revelation. See Paul Tillich, *The Protestant Era*, trans. James Luther Adams (Chicago: University of Chicago Press, 1948), pp. 27-31.
34. Hendrikus Berkhof, *Christian Faith*, trans. Sierd Woudstra (Grand Rapids: Eerdmans, 1979), p. 69.
35. See Arthur C. Cochrane, "On the Naming of God" (unpublished paper, University of Dubuque Theological Seminary, January 1984).
36. Robert W. Jenson, *The Triune Identity* (Philadelphia: Fortress Press, 1982), pp. 10-12. Jenson points out that *Yahweh* was the only proper name in ordinary use for Israel's God.

Chapter Three
God in Biblical Perspective

1. My position stands in diametrical opposition to that of both Pannenberg and Moltmann who express deep dissatisfaction with the God of classical Christian theism. Pannenberg says: "An almighty and omniscient being thought of as existing at the beginning of all temporal processes excludes freedom within the realm of his creation.... Freedom means the ability to go beyond a God who in some sense belongs to the totality of what exists." Wolfhart Pannenberg, *Basic Questions in*

Theology, trans. R.A. Wilson (London: SCM Press, 1973), 3: 108-9.

2. See Rudolf Otto, *The Idea of the Holy,* trans. John W. Harvey (New York: Oxford University Press, 1958), pp. 25-30.

3. George Maloney occasionally uses expressions like "the totally Other" and the "totally undefinable" to describe the God envisaged by the mystics of the Eastern Church. See George A. Maloney, *The Breath of the Mystic* (Denville, N.J.: Dimension Books, 1974), pp. 43, 44; idem, *Prayer of the Heart* (Notre Dame, Ind.: Ave Maria Press, 1981), p. 174.

4. See William J. Hill, *The Three-Personed God* (Washington, D.C.: Catholic University of America Press, 1982), pp. 241-72.

5. William Hill criticizes Barth for verging toward modalism, even while stopping short of it. See his *Three-Personed God,* pp. 111-28. I agree with Hill that we must not jettison the term "person" when applied to the Trinity but reinterpret it.

6. Vernard Eller, *The Language of Canaan and the Grammar of Feminism* (Grand Rapids: Eerdmans, 1982), p. 46.

7. It should be noted that the Hebrew language does not contain a specifically neuter gender, and therefore words with neuter meanings are necessarily represented either as masculine or feminine.

8. In this paragraph I am indebted to the personal assistance of Bruce Metzger of Princeton Theological Seminary; Joseph Mihelic of Dubuque Theological Seminary; and Frank Benz of Wartburg Theological Seminary.

   George Tavard maintains that the distinction between sex and gender persists in almost all known languages. While he admits that "'he' and 'she' usually correspond to male and female in English and American usage . . . this is due to a process of neutralization of everything that is not male or female ('it') and not to a primordial sexual status for 'he' or 'she.'" George H. Tavard, "Sexist Language in Theology?" *Woman: New Dimensions,* ed. Walter Burghardt (New York: Paulist Press, 1977), p. 130.

9. Karl Barth convincingly argues that the language of faith is based on the *analogia gratiae* (analogy of grace) in that it results from God's adoption of human language as his own. He opposes this to the *analogia entis* (analogy of being) in which we posit the attributes of God on the basis of the common denominator of being. For Barth, human language in and of itself is incapable of plumbing the depths of the mystery of God's trinitarian self-designation, but the Spirit of God may enter into our language and confer upon it the capacity to speak of God.

10. See W.A. Visser 't Hooft, *The Fatherhood of God in an Age of Emancipation* (Philadelphia: Westminster Press, 1982), pp. 119-27.

11. Robert Paul Roth, "The Problem of How to Speak of God," *Interpretation,* vol. 38, no. 1 (January 1984), p. 79.

12. Thomas F. Torrance, *Reality and Evangelical Theology,* p. 111.

13. Ibid.

14. Roth, "The Problem of How to Speak of God," p. 79.

15. P.T. Forsyth, *The Soul of Prayer* (London: Independent Press, 1966), p. 12.

16. The idea of church as mother was stoutly affirmed by both Luther and Calvin. It is even present in the Anabaptist tradition. Eberhard Arnold declares: "The Church, the virgin bride, who is our mother, comes to us, and all of life is transformed, including the economic structure." (*God's Revolution: The Witness of Eberhard Arnold,* ed. John Howard Yoder [New York: Paulist Press, 1984], p. 42.)

17. Tertullian, *De oratione,* c.2. cited in Henri de Lubac, *The Motherhood of the Church,* trans. Sr. Sergia Englund (San Francisco: Ignatius Press, 1982), p. 115. From my theological perspective, it is the Spirit as the soul of the church who guarantees that the names of the Father and the Son will be recognized and celebrated.

18. In Mark Gibbard, *Twentieth-Century Men of Prayer* (Naperville, Ill.: SCM Book Club, 1974), p. 34. Also, Henri de Lubac cites from a Russian journal these words of prayerful joy addressed to the Church: "Inestimable Mother, unforgettable Mother, radiant and all beautiful, Mother of sorrows, born on the Cross, you who give birth on the Cross, Mother of innumerable children, how sweet it is to meet you!" (*The Motherhood of the Church* [San Francisco: Ignatius Press, 1984], p. 84.)

19. See Rosemary Ruether, *Sexism and God-Talk,* pp. 47-52.

20. Ibid., pp. 38-41.

21. Paul D. Hanson, "Masculine Metaphors for God and Sex-Discrimination in the Old Testament," *The Ecumenical Review,* vol. 27, no. 4 (October, 1975), p. 318.

22. Cited in Visser't Hooft, *"The Fatherhood of God,* p. 131.

23. According to Visser't Hooft, "Gnosticism had, as it were, a place for woman in heaven as participating in creation, and a place in hell as the temptress responsible for man's imprisonment in sexuality. It had, however, no place for her as a person, as a human being on earth. It was therefore fundamentally opposed to marriage as a life-long covenant between two persons." (Ibid., p. 132.)

24. Merlin Stone, "The Three Faces of Goddess Spirituality," *The Politics of Women's Spirituality,* ed. Charlene Spretnak (New York: Doubleday & Co., 1982), pp. 69, 70.

Chapter Four
Resymbolizing the Faith

1. See Gail Ramshaw-Schmidt, "An Inclusive Language Lectionary," *Worship* 58 (1984): 35.

2. Starhawk, *The Spiral Dance: A Rebirth of the Ancient Religion of the Great Goddess* (San Francisco: Harper & Row, 1979), p. 9.

3. *Worship: Inclusive Language Resources* (St. Louis: Office for Church Life and Leadership, United Church of Christ, 1977), p. 30.

4. On Wieman's understanding of prayer, see Henry Nelson Wieman, *The Wrestle of Religion with Truth* (New York: Macmillan, 1927), pp. 68-82. Marjorie Suchocki sees prayer as a method for releasing redemptive possibilities into the world. See Marjorie Hewitt Suchocki, *God-Christ-*

Church: A Practical Guide to Process Theology (New York: Crossroad, 1982), pp. 205-206.

5. *An Inclusive Language Lectionary: Readings for Year A* (Cooperative Publication Association, John Knox Press, Westminster Press, Pilgrim Press, 1983), Pentecost 7.

6. Suchocki, *God-Christ-Church,* p. 215.

7. Susan Brooks Thistlethwaite, "God Language and the Trinity," *EKU-UCC Newsletter,* vol. 5, no. 1 (February 1984), p. 21.

8. Paul K. Jewett, *The Ordination of Women* (Grand Rapids: Eerdmans, 1980), p. 53.

9. John Dart, "Balancing Out the Trinity: The Genders of the Godhead," *The Christian Century* 100 (1983): 148. Joan Schaupp sets forth similar views in her *Woman: Image of the Holy Spirit* (Denville, N.J.: Dimension, 1975). Also see Leonard Swidler, "God the Father: Masculine; God the Son: Masculine; God the Holy Spirit: Feminine," *National Catholic Reporter,* January 31, 1975, pp. 7, 14; and Donald L. Gelpi, *The Divine Mother: A Trinitarian Theology of the Holy Spirit* (Lanham, Md.: University Press of America, 1984).

10. See "The Gnostic Connection" in chapter 1 (pp. 9-10).

11. Samuel Laeuchli, *The Language of Faith* (Nashville: Abingdon, 1962), p. 33. The author supports his critique by extensive references to original Gnostic writings.

12. Ibid., p. 34.

13. Rudolph, *Gnosis,* p. 64.

14. Jonas, *The Gnostic Religion,* p. 332.

15. Laeuchli, *Language of Faith,* p. 89.

16. Another suggested alternative, one that deflects from the historicity of the faith, is "Ground-Logos-Spirit." Robert Jenson scores such attempts to reformulate the Trinity as wrong-headed "parodies" and as "linguistically naive." Jenson, *The Triune Identity,* pp. 17, 20.

17. "Non-sexist Wording Denied," *Presbyterian Life and Times* (May 1984).

18. Harold Nebelsick, unpublished letter to Dr. Harold Daniels (Feb. 20, 1983), p. 6. Used with permission of the author.

19. Martha E. Stortz, "The Mother, the Son, and the Bullrushes: The Church and Feminist Theology," *Dialog,* vol. 23 (Winter, 1984), pp. 21-26.

20. Ibid., p. 25.

21. Ibid.

22. Virginia Mollenkott, *The Divine Feminine.*

23. Cited in Visser't Hooft, *The Fatherhood of God,* p. 133.

24. Ramshaw-Schmidt, "Lutheran Liturgical Prayer and God as Mother," p. 541. Another more questionable prayer suggested by Schmidt is the following: "O God our Father, our Mother and our nurse, in baptism you have given us life through the death of your Son. Feed us now with your bread and wine that we may receive and be his body in the world, through whom we pray."

25. For patristic allusions to divine maternity, see Ritamary Bradley,

"Patristic Background of the Motherhood Similitude in Julian of Norwich," *Christian Scholar's Review* 8 (1978): 101-13.

Chapter Five
The Problem of Authority

1. Rosemary Ruether, *Sexism and God-Talk,* p. 12. Ruether contends that what makes feminist theology unique is its appeal to women's experience.
2. Ibid., p. 13.
3. Ibid., p. 20.
4. Meinrad Craighead, "Immanent Mother," in Mary E. Giles, ed. *The Feminist Mystic and Other Essays on Women and Spirituality* (New York: Crossroad, 1982), p. 79. Similarly, Dorothee Sölle declares: "'Source of all that is good,' 'life-giving wind,' 'water of life,' 'light' are all symbols of God which do not imply power of authority and do not smack of any chauvinism." (*Beyond Mere Obedience,* trans. Lawrence W. Denef [New York: Pilgrim Press, 1982], p. xix.)
5. Spretnak, ed., *The Politics of Women's Spirituality,* p. xxiii.
6. Ibid., p. 416.
7. Ibid., p. 417.
8. Elisabeth Schüssler-Fiorenza, "Toward a Feminist Biblical Hermeneutics" in *Readings in Moral Theology No. 4,* ed. Charles E. Curran and Richard A. McCormick (New York: Paulist Press, 1984), p. 376. Also see Elisabeth Schüssler-Fiorenza, *In Memory of Her* (New York: Crossroad, 1983), pp. 4-67.
9. Fiorenza, "Toward a Feminist Biblical Hermeneutics," p. 378.
10. Ibid., pp. 376, 377. She is here citing Rachel Blau DuPlessis.
11. McFague, *Metaphorical Theology,* p. 59.
12. Ibid.
13. Ibid., p. 62.
14. Ibid.
15. Ibid.
16. Spretnak, ed., *The Politics of Women's Spirituality,* p. 73.
17. Ibid., p. 217.
18. Carl Olson, ed., *The Book of the Goddess Past and Present* (New York: Crossroad, 1983), pp. 217-30.
19. See Nadine Brozan, "In the Religious Life, a Conflict of Faith and Feminism," *New York Times* (March 8, 1980), p. 18.
20. This is made abundantly clear by Burton H. Throckmorton, Jr., in his "Why the Inclusive Language Lectionary?" *The Christian Century* 101 (1984): 742-44. Throckmorton appeals to "humanity's understanding of itself" as the norm by which to determine whether the Bible can be heard as the Word of God.
21. For the meaning of "opaque" in relation to "cloudy," "murky," and "turbid," see S.I. Hayakawa, ed., *Modern Guide to Synonymns and Related Words* (New York: Funk and Wagnalls, 1968), p. 227.

22. The fourteenth-century anonymous author of the mystical work *The Cloud of Unknowing*, trans. Clifton Wolters (Baltimore: Penguin Books, 1967), contends that we do not have real knowledge in the state of contemplation but only "a blind groping for the naked being of God" (p. 64). He acknowledges that God may on occasion "send out a shaft of spiritual light, which pierces this cloud of unknowing between you, and shows you some of his secrets, of which it is not permissible or possible to speak" (p. 87). *The Cloud of Unknowing* stands in the mystical tradition of pseudo-Dionysius who described God as "the Transcendent Darkness" that is "beyond being and knowing." In this kind of orientation, conceptual knowledge is replaced by a mystical silence.

23. Mysticism the world over denies that humans can have adequate conceptual knowledge of God. The names of God in mysticism are equivocal, since God is beyond essence, being, and intelligibility. See James F. Anderson, *The Bond of Being: An Essay on Analogy and Existence* (St. Louis: B. Herder Book Co., 1949), pp. 65, 66. Lao-tse says: "The name that can be named is not the enduring and unchanging name." *The Texts of Taoism*, trans. James Legge (New York: Julian Press, 1959), p. 95.

   This general orientation is reflected in Elizabeth A. Johnson, "The Incomprehensibility of God and the Image of God Male and Female," *Theological Studies*, vol. 45, no. 3 (Sept. 1984), pp. 441-65.

24. Clouser, who identifies "God's revelation" with sacred scripture, contends that religious language purports "to give univocal truth about God. It should not be seen as giving us something *like* what is true of God, while it is all really beyond our comprehension, as the analogy theorists maintain. Nor should it be understood as merely our resolve to talk about God *as if* he had such characteristics, as Kantians and pragmatists have maintained. Rather it should be seen as quite ordinary language purporting to ascribe to God properties which he really has and relations in which he really stands." Roy Clouser, "Religious Language: A New Look at an Old Problem" in Hendrik Hart, Johan Van Der Hoeven, and Nicholas Wolterstorff, eds., *Rationality in the Calvinian Tradition* (Lanham, Md.: University Press of America, 1983), pp. 394, 395.

25. See infra, pp. 103, 120 where I try to make a place for a univocal element in our basically analogical knowledge of God.

26. Gail Ramshaw-Schmidt, lecture at the Twin Cities Presbytery meeting, Hope Presbyterian Church, Richfield, Minn., May 8, 1984.

27. See Paul Ricoeur, *The Rule of Metaphor* (Toronto: University of Toronto Press, 1977), p. 291.

28. In my debate with Gail Ramshaw-Schmidt, she seemed open to this last suggestion.

29. Eckhart could say that God "is nonloving, being above love and affection." *Meister Eckhart*, ed. Raymond Blakney (New York: Harper, 1941), p. 248.

30. Karl Barth, *Church Dogmatics*, eds. G.W. Bromiley and T.F. Torrance,

trans. T.H.L. Parker, W.B. Johnston, Harold Knight, and J.L.M. Haire (Edinburgh: T. & T. Clark, repr. 1964), vol. 2, part 1, p. 213.

31. Lewis S. Ford, *The Lure of God* (Philadelphia: Fortress, 1978), p. 16.

32. Ibid., p. 135.

Chapter Six
Parallels with the German Christians

1. Harold Nebelsick, unpublished letter to Dr. Harold Daniels (Feb. 20, 1983).

2. Paul B. Means, *Things That Are Caesar's* (New York: Round Table Press, 1935), p. 180.

3. Cited in ibid., p. 170. See Alfred Rosenberg, *Der Mythus des 20. Jahrhunderts* (Munich: Hoheneichen Verlag, 1934), pp. 599-607.

4. In Adolf Keller, *Religion and the European Mind* (London: Lutterworth Press, 1934), p. 107.

5. Ibid., p. 108.

6. The Tannenberg Federation, like some of the other racist cults, criticized Protestant liberal theology from the left. It sought a pure Germanic-Aryan faith, a form of modern pantheism similar to the Indian world view. Mathilde Ludendorff, the cofounder with her husband General Erich Ludendorff, accused Jesus Christ of being guilty among other things of personal timidity and dishonesty in her book *Salvation from Jesus Christ* (1931). Her *The Great Displacement—the Bible Not God's Word* was a vituperative attack on the veracity of the Bible. It should also be kept in mind that the German Faith movements on the whole objected much more to political than to religious liberalism, for in a sense they represented the final culmination of liberal religious thought—mystical pantheism.

7. Arthur Frey, *Cross and Swastika* (London: Student Christian Movement Press, 1938), p. 83.

8. Ibid., p. 100.

9. Keller, *Religion and the European Mind*, p. 109.

10. Frey, *Cross and Swastika*, p. 121.

11. Ibid., p. 119.

12. Ibid.

13. Ibid., p. 129.

14. Keller, *Religion and the European Mind*, p. 114.

15. Frey, *Cross and Swastika*, p. 128.

16. Means, *Things That Are Caesar's*, p. 184.

17. Hermann Rauschning, *The Conservative Revolution* (New York: G.P. Putnam's Sons, 1941), pp. 255-56.

18. Salo Baron, *Modern Nationalism and Religion* (New York: Harper & Bros., 1947), p. 147.

19. Albert Richard Chandler, *Rosenberg's Nazi Myth* (Ithaca, N.Y.: Cornell University Press, 1945), p. 111.

20. Frey, *Cross and Swastika*, p. 142.

21. Ibid.

22. Ibid., p. 154.
23. Arthur C. Cochrane, *The Church's Confession under Hitler,* 2nd ed. (Pittsburgh, Penn.: Pickwick Press, 1976), pp. 94-95.
24. Rauschning, *The Conservative Revolution,* p. 181.
25. See Dale Vree, "Ideology versus Theology: Case Studies of Liberation Theology and the Christian New Right," in *Christianity Confronts Modernity,* ed. Peter Williamson and Kevin Perrotta (Ann Arbor, Mich.: Servant Books, 1981), pp. 57-78.
26. In their book *The Search for Christian America* (Westchester, Ill.: Crossway, 1983), authors Mark Noll, Nathan Hatch, and George Marsden dispute the widely held view that America's founding cultural consensus was distinctively Christian.
27. This does not apply to religious fundamentalism or the evangelical right, including Moral Majority, but it does apply to evangelicals as well as religious liberals caught up in the Positive Thinking and New Thought movements (which have a politically rightist hue). The evangelical right can nonetheless be charged with accommodating to the values and goals of American culture.
28. The New Thought movement is both unitarian and binitarian (they speak of the mother as well as of the father principle in God). When they do refer to the Trinity, they use such expressions as "Spirit, Soul, and Body" or "Mind, Idea, Consciousness," or something similar. See Charles S. Braden, *Spirits in Rebellion* (Dallas: Southern Methodist University Press, 1963); and *These Also Believe* (New York: Macmillan, 1949), pp. 78-220; 257-307.
29. See Constance E. Cumbey, *The Hidden Dangers of the Rainbow* (Shreveport, Louisiana: Huntington House, 1983); and Robert Burrows, "The New Age Movement," *Evangelical Newsletter,* vol. 11, no. 10 (May 11, 1984), pp. 3-4.
30. Rauschning, *The Conservative Revolution,* p. 197.
31. For the historical development of the term "ideology" beginning with the French Revolution, see Hans Barth, *Truth and Ideology,* trans. Frederic Lilge (Berkeley: University of California Press, 1976).
32. Hans Küng, *Does God Exist?* trans. Edward Quinn (N.Y.: Doubleday, 1980), p. 124.
33. See Peter Berger and Hansfried Kellner, *Sociology Reinterpreted* (New York: Doubleday Anchor Books, 1981), pp. 143-45.
34. Sheila Collins, *A Different Heaven and Earth* (Valley Forge, Penn.: Judson Press, 1974), p. 52.
35. Ruether, *Sexism and God-Talk,* p. 28.
36. Ibid., pp. 28-29.
37. Elisabeth Schüssler-Fiorenza, "Feminist Theology as a Critical Theology of Liberation" in *Woman: New Dimensions,* ed. Walter J. Burghardt (New York: Paulist Press, 1977), p. 40.
38. Elisabeth Schüssler-Fiorenza, "The Power of the Word," *The Review of Books and Religion,* vol. 12, no. 6 (March 1984), p. 5.
39. Harold Nebelsick, unpublished letter to Dr. Harold Daniels, February 20, 1983, p. 8.

Chapter Seven
The Growing Church Conflict

1. Clement of Alexandria dismissed the legitimacy of the biblical names for God on the basis that "the Divine Nature cannot be described as it really is" (*Stromata*, ii, 16). See Carl Henry's comments in his *God, Revelation, and Authority* (Waco, Texas: Word Books, 1976), 2:171.
2. Suchocki, *God-Christ-Church*.
3. Ibid., p. 215.
4. Ibid., p. 221.
5. Lewis S. Ford, *The Lure of God* (Philadelphia: Fortress, 1978), pp. 99-111.
6. See Hill, *The Three-Personed God*, p. 188.
7. See Karl Rahner, *The Trinity*, trans. Joseph Donceel (New York: Herder & Herder, 1970).
8. Moltmann, *The Trinity and the Kingdom*, p. 218.
9. Ibid., p. 60.
10. Moltmann, *The Crucified God*, trans. R.A. Wilson and John Bowden (New York: Harper & Row, 1974), pp. 246-47.
11. Wolfhart Pannenberg, *Basic Questions in Theology*, trans. George H. Kehm (Philadelphia: Westminster, 1983), 2:241.
12. Hill, *The Three-Personed God*, p. 161.
13. Ibid., p. 164.
14. Paul Tillich, *Systematic Theology*, 1:250.
15. Hill, *The Three-Personed God*, p. 96.
16. See Piet Schoonenberg, "Process or History in God?" *Theology Digest* 23 (Spring, 1975): 38-44.
17. John Macquarrie, *Principles of Christian Theology* (New York: Charles Scribner's Sons, 1966), p. 177.
18. Ibid.
19. Hill, *The Three-Personed God*, p. 147.
20. Susan Brooks Thistlethwaite, *Metaphors for the Contemporary Church* (New York: Pilgrim Press, 1983), p. 103.
21. Joseph A. Bracken, *What Are They Saying about the Trinity?* (New York: Paulist Press, 1979), p. 81.
22. McFague, *Metaphorical Theology*, p. 51.
23. Ruether, *Sexism and God-Talk*, p. 114.
24. Ibid., p. 138.
25. Ibid., p. 258.
26. John Macquarrie, *In Search of Humanity* (New York: Crossroad, 1983), p. 138.
27. Torrance, *Reality and Evangelical Theology*, p. 110.
28. Wieman, *The Wrestle of Religion with Truth*, pp. 223-26.
29. In my view it is not the symbol as such that informs theological thought but the Spirit of God acting in and through the symbol and sometimes even over against it.

30. Joseph Haroutunian, "Christian Faith and Metaphysics," *The Journal of Religion*, vol. 33 (1953): 103-112.
31. Ibid., p. 106.
32. Torrance, *Reality and Evangelical Theology*, p. 113.
33. Dietrich Bonhoeffer, *Christ the Center*, trans. John Bowden (New York: Harper & Row, 1966), pp. 91-92.
34. See Otto W. Heick, *A History of Christian Thought*, (Philadelphia: Fortress Press, 1965), 1: 379. With the aim of rendering the mystery of the Lord's Supper more intelligible, some theologians in the tradition of Lutheran orthodoxy came to positions known as consubstantiation (denoting a conjoining of the elements with the body and blood of Christ) and impanation (denoting a penetration of the body of Christ in the elements). Lutheran orthodoxy in general avoided this particular terminology.

    The emphasis of Luther was on the bodily presence of the person of Christ in the sacred meal whereas Melanchthon's stress was on the real personal presence of Christ. Both tried to stay clear of imagery that obscured or called into question the personal dimension of Christ's presence in the mystery of the Eucharist.
35. For a probing analysis of the theological implications of Ex 3:14 where God is defined in terms of a verb, see Adrio König, *Here Am I!* (Grand Rapids: Eerdmans, 1982), pp. 67-68. König suggests the translation, "I shall be what I was."
36. A Neoplatonic predilection can be discerned in the existentialist philosopher Berdyaev: "God is absolutely above all objectivization and he is not in any sense at all an object or objective being." Nicolas Berdyaev, *Truth and Revelation*, trans. R.M. French (New York: Collier Books, 1962), p. 56. Against Berdyaev I hold that God is objective in the sense that he exists apart from us and outside us, although we cannot encompass him in our objectification of him. I agree with Thomas Aquinas that God is that existent being whose essence is his existence.
37. Emil Brunner, *The Christian Doctrine of God*, trans. Olive Wyon (Philadelphia: Westminster Press, 1974), p. 206.
38. Ibid., p. 217, 227.
39. Though it is true that the Bible generally speaks of God as the Father of our Lord Jesus Christ rather than a universal Father of all humankind, there are some passages that point to the universality of the Fatherhood of God. At the same time, we must insist that we can know God as our personal Father only through faith in Jesus Christ. For a trenchant discussion of the particularistic and universalistic dimensions of the concept of God's Fatherhood in Ephesians, see Markus Barth, *Ephesians 1-3* (New York: Doubleday, 1974), pp. 379-84.

    The battle with Gnosticism is a potent reminder that simply calling God "Father" is not in itself a sign of true faith. Many of the Gnostics were not averse to using this designation, but they meant not the personal, concrete Father of biblical faith but the "first principle of the

All." Laeuchli says: "This 'Father', emptied of attributes, is no longer a Father in the biblical sense but the highest stage in a universe. He is a magnificent peak in religious ontology but not the personal Father of the gospel who provides love and judgment for his creatures." Laeuchli, *The Language of Faith,* p. 37.

40. John Macquarrie makes a good case that meaning involves a triadic relationship—the speaker, the matter on which he speaks and the hearer to whom he speaks. See *God-Talk* (New York: Harper & Row, 1967), pp. 64-68.

41. Suchocki, *God-Christ-Church,* p. 116.

42. One can say that the univocal element in our knowledge of God is God's knowledge of us, in which we participate but which we can never objectify or delineate as something separate from our knowledge. God's perfect knowledge of us is hidden in our imperfect knowledge of him. Only in the eschatological consummation will we know even as we are known (1 Cor 13:12).

43. For example, we can know God's love, agape, literally when it rains down upon us, but this is an ecstatic, not a theoretical knowledge. As soon as we try to understand it and express it, we are thinking analogically or symbolically. We can say that agape is unconditional and sacrificial, but the full meaning of these words remains veiled to us. The light we can bring to these words comes not from the ordinary understanding of them but from faith's perception of the mystery of God's sacrifice for us in the life and death of Jesus Christ.

44. I reject the argument of existentialist theologians that we can only have a nonobjective knowledge of God because God is not an object for our understanding. I agree with Barth that although we cannot objectify God, God can objectify himself; he can make himself an object for our understanding. But this word from God is never at our disposal, and that is why it must be given to us ever again.

45. Cf. Bonhoeffer: "An idea is universally accessible, it is already there. Man can appropriate it of his own free will" (*Christ the Center,* p. 51). If God or Christ were reduced to an idea, he would then be a timeless truth and not a living or personal God.

46. On the relation between synecdoche, metonomy, and metaphor see Gracia Grindal, "Reflections on God the Father," *Word & World,* vol. 4, no. 1 (Winter, 1984), pp. 76-86.

Publications of
Donald Bloesch
1953-1985

Books: Author or Editor

Centers of Christian Renewal. Philadelphia: United Church Press, 1964.

The Christian Life and Salvation. Grand Rapids: William B. Eerdmans Publishing Co., 1967.

The Crisis of Piety. Grand Rapids: William B. Eerdmans Publishing Co., 1968.

The Christian Witness in a Secular Age. Minneapolis: Augsburg Publishing House, 1968.

Christian Spirituality East and West. Chicago: Priory Press, 1968. (Co-author)

The Reform of the Church. Grand Rapids: Wm. B. Eerdmans Publishing Co., 1970.

The Ground of Certainty: Toward an Evangelical Theology of Revelation. Grand Rapids: William B. Eerdmans Publishing Co., 1971.

Servants of Christ: Deaconesses in Renewal. Minneapolis: Bethany Fellowship, 1971. (Editor)

The Evangelical Renaissance. Grand Rapids: William B. Eerdmans Publishing Co., 1973; London: Hodder & Stoughton, 1974.

Wellsprings of Renewal: Promise in Christian Communal Life. Grand Rapids: William B. Eerdmans Publishing Co., 1974.

Light a Fire. St. Louis: Eden Publishing House, 1975.

The Invaded Church. Waco, Texas: Word Books, 1975.

Jesus Is Victor!: Karl Barth's Doctrine of Salvation. Nashville: Abingdon Press, 1976.

The Orthodox Evangelicals. Nashville: Thomas Nelson, 1978. (Co-editor)

Essentials of Evangelical Theology. Vol. 1. *God, Authority and Salvation.* San Francisco: Harper & Row, 1978.
Essentials of Evangelical Theology. Vol. 2. *Life, Ministry and Hope.* San Francisco: Harper & Row, 1979.
The Struggle of Prayer. San Francisco: Harper & Row, 1980.
Faith and its Counterfeits. Downers Grove, Ill.: InterVarisity Press, 1981.
Is the Bible Sexist? Westchester, Ill.: Crossway Books, 1982.
The Future of Evangelical Christianity. New York: Doubleday, 1983.
Crumbling Foundations. Grand Rapids: Zondervan Publishing House, 1984.
The Battle for the Trinity. Ann Arbor: Servant Books, 1985.

Books: Contributor

"Rethinking the Church's Mission" in *Berufung und Bewährung: Internationale Festschrift für Erik Wickberg,* ed. J.W. Winterhager and Arnold Brown. Giessen, Basel: Brunnen Verlag, 1974. English title: *Vocation and Victory.*
"The Basic Issue," in *Christ Is Victor,* ed. W. Glyn Evans, pp. 27-30. Valley Forge, Pa.: Judson Press, 1977.
"A Call to Spirituality," in *The Orthodox Evangelicals,* ed. Robert Webber and Donald Bloesch, pp. 146-65. Nashville: Nelson, 1978.
"Scriptural Primacy" in *Issues in Sexual Ethics,* ed. Martin Duffy, pp. 27-35. Souderton, Pa.: United Church People for Biblical Witness, 1979.
"The Challenge Facing the Churches" in *Christianity Confronts Modernity,* ed. Peter Williamson and Kevin Perrotta, pp. 205-23. Ann Arbor, Michigan: Servant Books, 1981.
"Pietism" in *Beacon Dictionary of Theology,* ed. Richard S. Taylor. Kansas City, Mo.: Beacon Hill Press, 1983.
"Sin, Atonement, and Redemption" in *Evangelicals and Jews in an Age of Pluralism,* ed. Marc H. Tanenbaum, Marvin R. Wilson, and A. James Rudin, pp. 163-82. Grand Rapids: Baker Book House, 1984.
"Conversion" in *Evangelical Dictionary of Theology,* ed. Walter Elwell. Grand Rapids: Baker Book House, 1984.
"Descent into Hell (Hades)" in *Evangelical Dictionary of Theology,* 1984.

"Fate" in *Evangelical Dictionary of Theology*, 1984.
"Moral Rearmament" in *Evangelical Dictionary of Theology*, 1984.
"Peter T. Forsyth" in *Evangelical Dictionary of Theology*, 1984.
"Prayer" in *Evangelical Dictionary of Theology*, 1984.
"Sin" in *Evangelical Dictionary of Theology*, 1984.
"A Christological Hermeneutic" in *The Use of the Bible in Theology: Evangelical Options*, ed. Robert K. Johnston. Atlanta: John Knox Press, 1985.
"Process Theology and Reformed Theology" in *Process Theology*, ed. Ronald Nash. Milford, Mich.: Mott Media, 1986.

Articles and Book Reviews

"Theology and Philosophy." *Quest*, Spring, 1952, pp. 1-10. Published by the University of Chicago Divinity School.
"The Flight from God." *Witness*, vol. 1, no. 1 (February 1953), pp. 6, 7.
"Theology and Psychotherapy." *Witness*, vol. 2, no. 1 (October 1953), pp. 7-10.
"The Bible, Plato, and the Reformers." A review of W.P. Witcutt, *The Rise and Fall of the Individual. Interpretation*, vol. 13, no. 2 (April 1959), pp. 219-21.
"Creation as Event." A review of Karl Barth, *The Doctrine of Creation*, vol. 3, part 1 of Barth's *Church Dogmatics. The Christian Century* vol. 76, no. 37 (September 16, 1959), pp. 1055, 1056.
"The Christian and the Drift Towards War." *Theology and Life*, vol. 2, no. 4 (November 1959), pp. 318-26.
Reviews of A. Gabriel Hebert, *Fundamentalism and the Church* and J.I. Packer, *"Fundamentalism" and the Word of God. Religion in Life*, vol. 29, no. 1 (Winter, 1959-60), pp. 154, 155.
"Defender of Free Grace." Reviews of Ronald Knox, trans., *Autobiography of St. Thérèse of Lisieux* and Ida F. Görres, *The Hidden Face. The Christian Century*, vol. 77, no. 11 (March 16, 1960), p. 318.
Review of Everett Knight, *The Objective Society. The Presbyterian Outlook*, vol. 142, no. 13 (March 28, 1960), p. 15.
"Billy Graham: A Theological Appraisal." *Theology and Life*, vol. 3, no. 2 (May 1960), pp. 136-43.
"Biblical Religion vs. Culture Religion." *Theology and Life*, vol. 3, no. 3 (August 1960), pp. 175-76.

"Nothing Ventured." A review of John H. Gerstner, *Reasons for Faith*. In *The Christian Century*, vol. 77, no. 42 (October 19, 1960), pp. 1217-18. For a slightly modified version, see *Theology and Life*, vol. 3, no. 4 (November 1960), pp. 331, 332.

"Love Illuminated." A review of C.S. Lewis, *The Four Loves*. The *Christian Century*, vol. 77, no. 50 (December 14, 1960), p. 1470.

Review of Georgia Harkness, *The Providence of God. Interpretation*, vol. 15, no. 1 (January 1961), pp. 106, 107.

"Syncretism: Its Cultural Forms and Its Influence." *Dubuque Christian American*, vol. 36, no. 2 (May 1961), p. 2.

"World-Relatedness." A review of Paul S. Minear, *Images of the Church in the New Testament. The Christian Century*, vol. 78, no. 32 (August 9, 1961), pp. 958, 959.

"Vain Hope for Victory" in *The Pulpit* vol. 32, no. 11 (November 1961), pp. 9-11. Published by The Christian Century Foundation.

Review of Hilda Graef, *The Word of God in the World Today. The Presbyterian Outlook*, vol. 143, no. 45 (December 11, 1961), p. 15.

"The Christian Life in the Plan of Salvation." *Theology and Life*, vol. 5, no. 4 (November 1962), pp. 299-308.

Review of *A Kierkegaard Critique*, ed. Howard Johnson and Niels Thulstrup. *The Presbyterian Outlook*, vol. 144, no. 40 (November 5, 1962), p. 15.

"Virgin Birth Defended." A review of Thomas Boslooper, *The Virgin Birth. The Christian Century* vol. 80, no. 16 (April 17, 1963), pp. 493, 494.

Review of Arthur B. Crabtree, *The Restored Relationship. The Pulpit*, vol. 35, no. 3 (March 1964), pp. 27-28.

"A Name for Your Church." *United Church Herald*, vol. 7, no. 10 (May 15, 1964), pp. 18, 19.

Review of Langdon Gilkey, *How the Church Can Minister to the World without Losing Itself. The Presbyterian Outlook*, vol. 147, no. 14 (April 5, 1965), p. 15.

"The Divine Sacrifice." *Theology and Life*, vol. 8, no. 3 (Fall, 1965), pp. 192-202.

Review of Bela Vassady, *Christ's Church: Evangelical, Catholic, and Reformed. Theology and Life*, vol. 8, no. 3 (Fall, 1965), pp. 238-40.

"Spiritual Ecumenism." A review of Otto Piper, *Protestantism in an Ecumenical Age*. *The Christian Century*, vol. 82, no. 47 (November 24, 1965), pp. 1450, 1451.

Review of *Ultimate Concern: Tillich in Dialogue*. *Christian Advocate*, vol. 10, no. 1 (January 13, 1966), p. 20.

Review of Ernest B. Koenker, *Secular Salvations*. *The Presbyterian Outlook*, vol. 148, no. 7 (February 14, 1966), p. 15.

"Prophetic Preaching and Civil Rights." *The Pulpit*, vol. 37, no. 2 (February 1966), pp. 7-9.

"A Theology of Christian Commitment." *Theology and Life*, vol. 9, no. 4 (Winter, 1966), pp. 335-44.

"The Confession and the Sacraments." *Monday Morning*, vol. 31, no. 6 (March 14, 1966), pp. 6-8.

"The Charismatic Revival: A Theological Critique." *Religion in Life*, vol. 35, no. 3 (Summer, 1966), pp. 364-80.

"The Secular Theology of Harvey Cox." *The Dubuque Seminary Journal*, vol. 1, no. 2 (Fall, 1966), pp. 1-4.

Reviews of Paul Tillich, *On the Boundary* and *The Future of Religions*. *Christian Advocate*, vol. 10, no. 19 (October 6, 1966), p. 19.

"The Crisis of Piety." *The Covenant Quarterly*, vol. 25, no. 1 (February 1967), pp. 3-11.

"The Pilgrimage of Faith." *Encounter*, vol. 28, no. 1 (Winter, 1967), pp. 47-62.

Review of Dietrich Bonhoeffer, *Christ the Center*. *The Presbyterian Outlook*, vol. 149, no. 11 (March 13, 1967), p. 15.

"The Constitution on Divine Revelation" [A Reader's Response]. *Journal of Ecumenical Studies*, vol. 4, no. 3 (Summer, 1967), pp. 550, 551.

"Catholic Theology Today." Review of Karl Rahner, *Theological Investigations Vol. IV*. *Christianity Today*, vol. 12, no. 3 (November 10, 1967), pp. 38, 39.

"An Exposé of the New Factory Farms." *The Catholic Worker* (November 1967). Republished in *NCSAW Report*, February 1968.

Review of Oscar Cullmann, *Salvation in History*. *Christian Advocate*, vol. 11, no. 25 (December 28, 1967), p. 16.

"What's Wrong with the Liturgical Movement?" *Christianity Today*, vol. 12, no. 7 (January 5, 1968), pp. 6, 7.

Review of *The Sacraments: An Ecumenical Dilemma*, ed. Hans Küng. *Journal of Ecumenical Studies*, vol. 5, no. 2 (Spring, 1968), pp. 391, 392.

"Church Funds for Revolution?" [An editorial]. *Christianity Today*, vol. 12, no. 15 (April 26, 1968), pp. 27, 28.

"The Meaning of Conversion." *Christianity Today*, vol. 12, no. 17 (May 24, 1968), pp. 8, 10.

Review of Frank Stagg, E. Glenn Hinson, and Wayne Oates, *Glossolalia: Tongue Speaking in Biblical, Historical, and Psychological Perspective. Religion in Life*, vol. 37, no. 2 (Summer, 1968), pp. 308, 309.

"Intensive Farming." *Lutheran Forum*, vol. 2, no. 7 (July 1968), pp. 4-6.

"Thielicke's Ethics: A Review Article." *The Lutheran Quarterly*, vol. 20, no. 3 (August 1968), pp. 309-13.

"This Immoral War" [pamphlet] University of Dubuque, 1968.

Review of Augustin Cardinal Bea, *The Way to Unity after the Council* and George Caird, *Our Dialogue with Rome. Journal of the American Academy of Religion*, vol. 36, no. 3 (September 1968), pp. 287-89.

"The Need for Biblical Preaching." *The Reformed Journal*, vol. 19, no. 1 (January 1969), pp. 11-14.

"Fractured Theology." *The Reformed Journal*, vol. 19, no. 2 (February, 1969), pp. 14-16.

"Why People Are Leaving the Churches." *Religion in Life*, vol. 38, no. 1 (Spring, 1969), pp. 92-101.

Review of Arthur Vogel, *Is the Last Supper Finished? Secular Light on a Sacred Meal. The Presbyterian Outlook*, vol. 151, no. 13 (March 31, 1969), p. 15.

"Historicist Theology." A review of Gordon Kaufman, *Systematic Theology: A Historicist Perspective. Christianity Today*, vol. 13, no. 20 (July 4, 1969), pp. 16, 17.

"Can Gospel Preaching Save the Day?" *Eternity*, vol. 20, no. 7 (July, 1969), pp. 6-8, 33.

"Martyred for Christ." *Presbyterian Life*, vol. 22, no. 15 (August 1, 1969), pp. 34, 35.

Review of H.M. Kuitert, *The Reality of Faith. Encounter*, vol. 30, no. 3 (Summer, 1969), pp. 272-74.

"Syncretism and Social Involvement." A review of Harold Brown,

The Protest of a Troubled Protestant. Eternity, vol. 20, no. 10 (October 1969), pp. 44, 45.

"Evangelical Confession." *Dialog,* vol. 9, no. 1 (Winter, 1970), pp. 26-34.

"Is Christianity a Comedy?" A review of Harvey Cox, *The Feast of Fools. Eternity,* vol. 21, no. 4 (April 1970), pp. 59, 60.

Review of William Kuhns, *In Pursuit of Dietrich Bonhoeffer.* In *Religious Education,* vol. 65, no. 3 (May-June 1970), pp. 279, 280.

Review of Ian Henderson, *Power without Glory. Encounter,* vol. 31, no. 3 (Summer, 1970), pp. 283, 284.

"A Catholic Theologian Speaks." Review of Karl Rahner, *Theological Investigations Vol. VI. Christianity Today,* vol. 14, no. 20 (July 3, 1970), pp. 26-28.

"True and False Ecumenism." *Christianity Today,* vol. 14, no. 21 (July 17, 1970), pp. 3-5.

"Decision and Risk." Review of James Angell, *Put Your Arms around the City* and Keith Miller, *Habitation of Dragons. The Christian Century,* vol. 88, no. 4 (January 27, 1971), pp. 133-35.

Review of Jacques Ellul, *To Will and To Do. Eternity,* vol. 22, no. 4 (April 1971), p. 50.

"The Meaning of Salvation." *Good News,* vol. 4, no. 4 (April-June 1971), pp. 53-57.

"Heaven's Warning to Earth's Pride." *Eternity,* vol. 22, no. 5 (May 1971), pp. 12, 13, 45-47.

"Burying the Gospel, Part I." *Christianity Today,* vol. 15, no. 25 (September 24, 1971), pp. 8-11.

"Burying the Gospel, Part II." *Christianity Today,* vol. 16, no. 1 (October 8, 1971), pp. 12-14.

"'Christian' Radical?" Review of Jackson Lee Ice, *Schweitzer: Prophet of Radical Theology. The Christian Century,* vol. 88, no. 44 (Nov. 3, 1971), p. 1296

"The Misunderstanding of Prayer" in *The Christian Century,* vol. 88, no. 51 (Dec. 22, 1971), pp. 1492-94.

"New Wind Rising." Review of *Theology of the Liberating Word,* ed. Frederick Herzog. *Christianity Today,* vol. 16, no. 9 (February 4, 1972), p. 17.

"Child Communion as a Means of Cheap Grace." *Monday Morning,* vol. 37, no. 5 (March 6, 1972), pp. 3-5.

"Unrestricted Communion." *The Presbyterian Journal,* vol. 30, no. 50

(April 12, 1972), pp. 12-13. Reprint of March 6 *Monday Morning* article.

"Salvation as Justice." Review of Johannes Verkuyl, *The Message of Liberation in Our Age. The Christian Century,* vol. 89, no. 26 (July 5-12, 1972), pp. 751-52.

"The Ideological Temptation." *Listening,* vol. 7, no. 1 (Winter, 1972), pp. 45-54.

"The New Evangelicalism." *Religion in Life,* vol. 41, no. 3 (Autumn, 1972), pp. 327-39.

"Key 73: Pathway to Renewal?" *The Christian Century,* vol. 90, no. 1 (Jan. 3, 1973), pp. 9-11.

"Catholic Ferment." A review of David F. Wells, *Revolution in Rome. The Christian Century,* vol. 90, no. 6 (Feb. 7, 1973), pp. 184-86.

"What Kind of Bread Do We Give Them?" *Eternity,* vol. 24, no. 3 (March 1973), pp. 37-49. An expansion and revision of the essay on salvation published in *Good News,* vol. 4, no. 4. Republished under the title "Significato di Salvezza" in the Italian ecumenical journal, *Vivere In* Anno 1, no. 4 (July-August 1973), pp. 20-22.

"The Missing Dimension." *Reformed Review,* vol. 26, no. 3 (Spring, 1973), pp. 162-68, 179-88.

Review of Jaroslav Pelikan, *The Christian Tradition* Vol. I. *Journal of Ecumenical Studies,* vol. 10, no. 4 (Fall, 1973), pp. 801-3.

"The Wind of the Spirit." *The Reformed Journal,* vol. 23, no. 8 (October 1973), pp. 11-16.

"Ramm Reaffirms Our Great Heritage." A review of Bernard Ramm's *The Evangelical Heritage. Eternity,* vol. 25, no. 1 (January 1974), p. 36.

Review of H.P. Owen, *Concepts of Deity* and James Daane, *The Freedom of God. The Reformed Journal,* vol. 24, no. 2 (February 1974), p. 23.

"Rethinking Mission." Review of John Cobb, *Liberal Christianity at the Crossroads* and Robert McAfee Brown, *Frontiers for the Church Today. The Christian Century,* vol. 91, no. 7 (Feb. 20, 1974), pp. 211, 212.

"Hardness of Heart." *Cross Talk,* vol. 3, no. 3 (Fall, 1974). Adult Sunday School Curriculum of the United Methodist Church.

"Whatever Became of Neo-Orthodoxy?" *Christianity Today,* vol. 19, no. 5 (December 6, 1974), pp. 7-12.

"A New Tribalism." Review of Robert Harvey's *The Restless Heart.*

Christianity Today, vol. 19, no. 8 (January 17, 1975), p. 32.

"To Build Bridges." Review of Avery Dulles, *Models of the Church. The Christian Century,* vol. 92, no. 4 (Jan. 29, 1975), pp. 89-91.

"Moltmann's Crucified God." *Communio,* vol. 2, no. 4 (Winter, 1975), pp. 413, 414.

"What Troubles Christendom?" *His,* vol. 35, no. 5 (February 1975), pp. 18-21.

"Where the Church Touches the World." *His,* vol. 35, no. 6 (March 1975), pp. 12-14.

"New Enlightenment." Comparative review of George H. Smith, *Atheism: The Case against God* and Algernon D. Black, *Without Burnt Offerings. The Christian Century,* vol. 92, no. 12 (April 2, 1975), pp. 339.

"The Basic Issue." *Decision,* vol. 16, no. 11 (November 1975), p. 4.

Review of Helmut Thielicke, *The Evangelical Faith. Eternity,* vol. 26, no. 11 (November, 1975), pp. 51, 52.

"What's Behind the Manson Cult?" Review of R.C. Zaehner, *Our Savage God. Christianity Today,* vol. 20, no. 5 (December 5, 1975), p. 35.

"Wind of the Spirit." Review of *Aspects of Pentecostal-Charismatic Origins* ed. Vinson Synan and James D.G. Dunn, *Jesus and the Spirit. The Review of Books and Religion,* vol. 5, no. 11 (Mid-February 1976), p. 11.

"A Righteous Nation." *Crosstalk,* vol. 1, no. 5, part 1 (March-April-May 1976).

"Prayer and Mysticism (1): Two Types of Spirituality." *The Reformed Journal,* vol. 26, no. 3 (March 1976), pp. 23-26.

"Prayer and Mysticism (2): Divergent Views on Prayer." *The Reformed Journal,* vol. 26, no. 4 (April 1976), pp. 22-25.

"Prayer and Mysticism (3): Towards Renewed Evangelical Prayer." *The Reformed Journal,* vol. 26, no. 5 (May-June 1976), pp. 20-22.

"Options in Current Theology." Review of John Macquarrie, *Thinking about God. Christianity Today,* vol. 20, no. 14 (April 9, 1976), pp. 39, 40.

Review of Jacques Ellul, *The New Demons. Eternity,* vol. 27, no. 9 (September 1976), pp. 53, 54.

Review of David F. Wells and John D. Woodbridge, eds. *The Evangelicals. Christian Scholar's Review,* vol. 6, no. 1 (1976), pp. 81-83.

"An Evangelical Views the New Catholicism." *Communio,* vol. 3, no. 3 (Fall, 1976), pp. 215-30.

"True Spirituality." Review of Bernhard Christensen, *The Inward Pilgrimage. Christianity Today,* vol. 21, no. 2 (October 22, 1976), pp. 44, 45.

A review of Langdon Gilkey, *Catholicism Confronts Modernity. Eternity,* vol. 28, no. 1 (January 1977), pp. 56-58.

"Biblical Piety vs. Religiosity." *Religion in Life,* vol. 46, no. 4 (Winter, 1977), pp. 488-96.

"Christian Humanism." Review of Hans Kung, *On Being a Christian Christianity Today,* vol. 21, no. 15 (May 6, 1977), pp. 50, 51.

"Defender of Evangelicalism." Review of Helmut Thielicke, *The Evangelical Faith,* vol. 2. *The New Review of Books and Religion,* vol. 1, no. 10 (June 1977), p. 6.

"The Mystical Side of Luther." Review of Bengt R. Hoffman. *Luther and the Mystics. Christianity Today,* vol. 21, no. 20 (July 29, 1977), p. 30.

"The Pilgrimage of Karl Barth." Review of Eberhard Busch, *Karl Barth: His Life from Letters and Autobiographical Texts. Christianity Today,* vol. 22, no. 2 (October 21, 1977), pp. 35, 36.

"Breakthrough into Freedom." *The Presbyterian Journal,* vol. 36, no. 29 (November 16, 1977), pp. 7-8, 19-20.

"The Church: Catholic and Apostolic." Review of G.C. Berkouwer, *The Church. Christianity Today,* vol. 22, no. 5 (December 9, 1977), pp. 46, 47.

"Creative Transcendence." Review of Ray Sherman Anderson, *Historical Transcendence and the Reality of God. The Reformed Journal,* vol. 28, no. 12 (December 1977), p. 30.

"A Subversive Act." Review of *Thy Will Be Done: Praying the Our Father as Subversive Activity. The Christian Century,* vol. 95, no. 6 (Feb. 22, 1978), pp. 195, 196.

Review of Carl F.H. Henry, *God, Revelation and Authority,* vols. 1 and 2. *Reformed Review,* vol. 31, no. 2 (Winter, 1978), pp. 93-95.

"Tensions in the Church." Review of Jurgen Moltmann, *The Church in the Power of the Spirit. Christianity Today,* vol. 22, no. 14 (April 12, 1978), pp. 36-39.

Review of Karl Barth, *Final Testimonies. New Oxford Review,* vol. 45, no. 5 (May 1978), pp. 21, 22.

"A Bleak Outlook." Review of Jacques Ellul, *The Betrayal of the West.*

In *The Christian Century,* vol. 95, no. 27 (Aug. 30-Sept. 6, 1978), pp. 801, 802.

"Toward a Catholic Evangelical Understanding of the Lord's Supper." *Spirituality Today,* vol. 30, no. 3 (September 1978), pp. 236-49.

"Crisis in Biblical Authority." *Theology Today,* vol. 35, no. 4 (January 1979), pp. 455-62.

Review of Paul Holmer, *The Grammar of Faith. Eternity,* vol. 30, no. 3 (March 1979), pp. 50-52.

"Donald G. Bloesch Replies." *New Oxford Review,* vol. 46, no. 4 (May 1979), pp. 10, 11. A response to Canon Francis W. Read on The Chicago Call.

Review of Geoffrey W. Bromiley, *Historical Theology: An Introduction. Theology Today,* vol. 36, no. 3 (October 1979), pp. 452, 453.

"Process Theology in Reformed Perspective." *Listening,* vol. 14, no. 3 (Fall, 1979), pp. 185-95. Published concurrently in a slightly altered version in *The Reformed Journal,* vol. 29, no. 10 (October 1979), pp. 19-24.

"A Catholic Examination of the Basics." A review of Karl Rahner, *Foundations of the Christian Faith. Christianity Today,* vol. 23, no. 25 (November 2, 1979), p. 50.

Review of Dale Brown, *Understanding Pietism. TSF News and Reviews,* vol. 3, no. 2 (November 1979), p. 11.

A response to "Theological Education and Liberation Theology" by Frederick Herzog, et al. *Theological Education,* vol. 16, no. 1 (Autumn, 1979), pp.16-19.

"Postmodern Orthodoxy." Review of Thomas C. Oden, *Agenda for Theology. Christianity Today,* vol. 24, no. 6 (March 21, 1980), p. 37. Republished in *Pastoral Renewal,* vol. 5, no. 5 (November 1980), pp. 38c-38d.

"The Sword of the Spirit: The Meaning of Inspiration." *Reformed Review,* vol. 33, no. 2 (Winter, 1980), pp. 65-72. Also published in *Themelios,* vol. 5, no. 3 (May 1980), pp. 14-19.

"Rationalism." A review of Carl Henry, *God, Revelation and Authority,* vols. 3 and 4. *The Christian Century,* vol. 97, no. 13 (April 9, 1980), pp. 414, 415.

"Hartshorne, Barth, and Process Theology." A review of Colin E. Gunton, *Becoming and Being. The Reformed Journal,* vol. 30, no. 5 (May 1980), pp. 31, 32.

"Liturgical Sexism: A New Dispute." *Eternity,* vol. 31, no. 6 (June 1980), p. 13.

"To Reconcile the Biblically Oriented." *The Christian Century,* vol. 97, no. 24 (July 16-23, 1980), pp. 733-35.

"What Think Ye of Christ? A Test." *Christianity Today,* vol. 24, no. 15 (September 5, 1980), p. 25.

"How the 20th Century Is Eroding the Christian Message." A review of Harry Blamires, *The Secularist Heresy. Pastoral Renewal,* vol. 5, no. 5 (November 1980), pp. 38d-38e.

Review of Gerd Theissen, *A Critical Faith. Interpretation,* vol. 35, no. 1 (January 1981), pp. 102, 103.

"Reflections on Intercommunion." *Living Faith,* vol. 1, no. 4 (Winter, 1981), pp. 13-17.

"Soteriology in Contemporary Christian Thought." *Interpretation,* vol. 35, no. 2 (April 1981), pp. 132-44.

"Traditional Roles Defended." Review of Stephen Clark, *Man and Woman in Christ. Christianity Today,* vol. 26, no. 7 (April 24, 1981), p. 56.

"What Kind of People?" *A.D.* Magazine, vol. 10, no. 5 (May 1981), pp. 18-20. Two separate essays for United Church of Christ and United Presbyterian editions.

Review of *Essentials of Wesleyan Theology* by Paul A. Mickey. *Eternity,* vol. 32, no. 7-8 (July-August 1981), pp. 33, 34.

"The Reformers Shed the Shackles of Legalism." *Christianity Today,* vol. 25, no. 18 (October 23, 1981), pp. 18-20.

"Peril and Opportunity in the Church Today." *Center Journal,* vol 1, no. 1 (Winter, 1981), pp. 14-17. Published concurrently in *Living Faith,* vol. 2, no. 3 (Fall, 1981), pp. 3-5. Republished in *The Presbyterian Layman,* vol. 15, no. 2 (March-April 1982), pp. 11, 12.

"Karl Barth and the Life of the Church." *Center Journal,* vol. 1, no. 1 (Winter, 1981), pp. 65-77.

"Is Concern over Heresy Outdated?" *Eternity,* vol 32, no. 11 (November 1981), pp. 16, 17. Republished in *Good News,* vol. 16, no. 2 (September-October 1982), pp. 67-70.

"A Discussion of Hans Küng's, *Does God Exist?*" *Dialog,* vol. 20, no. 4 (Fall, 1981), pp. 317-21.

Review of Geoffrey Bromiley, *Historical Theology: An Introduction. Living Faith,* vol. 2, no. 3 (Fall, 1981), pp. 27-28. Note: This is a fresh review of this book and is not a duplicate of the review published earlier in *Theology Today.*

"Rethinking Monotheism." Review of Jürgen Moltmann, *The Trinity and the Kingdom. The Reformed Journal,* vol. 31, no. 11 (November-December 1981), pp. 29, 30.

"Karl Barth Speaks Again on Piety and Morality, Logos and Praxis." Review of Karl Barth, *Ethics. The Review of Books and Religion,* vol. 10, no. 3 (Mid-November 1981), p. 9.

"Secular Humanism—Not the Only Enemy." *Eternity,* vol. 33, no. 1 (January 1982), p. 22.

Review of *The Fundamentalist Phenomenon,* ed. Jerry Falwell with Ed Dobson and Ed Hindson. *New Oxford Review,* vol. 49, no. 3 (April 1982), p. 24.

"Encountering Systematics as an Evangelical." *Catalyst,* vol. 2, no. 2 (February 1982), pp. 1-3.

Review of *The Atoning Gospel* by James E. Tull. *TSF Bulletin,* vol. 6, no. 2 (November-December 1982), p. 23. Published concurrently in *Interpretation,* vol. 37, no. 1 (January 1983), pp. 106-7.

Review of David Tracy, *The Analogical Imagination. TSF Bulletin,* vol. 6, no. 3 (January-February 1983), pp. 23-24.

Review of M. Eugene Osterhaven, *The Faith of the Church. The Presbyterian Outlook,* vol. 165, no. 7 (February 14, 1983), p. 14.

Review of Richard Quebedeaux, *By What Authority. New Oxford Review,* vol. 1, no. 4 (May 1983), pp. 31-32.

"Many Barth Letters." Reviews of Karl Barth, *Letters 1961-1968,* and *Karl Barth and Rudolf Bultmann: Letters, 1922-1966. The Review of Books and Religion,* vol. 11, no. 8 (Mid-May 1983), p. 9.

"But Should We Be Ordained?" A review of Marjorie Warkentin, *Ordination: A Biblical-Historical View. Eternity,* vol. 34, no. 7 (July-August 1983), p. 38.

"Apocalyptic and Last Things." A review of Christopher Rowland, *The Open Heaven: A Study of Apocalyptic in Judaism and Early Christianity. The Review of Books and Religion,* vol. 12, no. 1 (Mid-September 1983), p. 6.

"Donald Bloesch Responds." A reply to Clark Pinnock. *Evangelical Newsletter,* vol. 10, no. 20 (October 28, 1983), p. 3.

Review of Avery Dulles, *Models of Revelation. The Christian Century* vol. 100, no. 34 (Nov. 16, 1983), pp. 1057, 1058.

" 'Evangelical': Integral to Christian Identity? An Exchange between

Donald Bloesch and Vernard Eller." *TSF Bulletin,* vol. 7, no. 2 (November-December 1983), pp. 5-10.

Review of Bernard Ramm, *After Fundamentalism: The Future of Evangelical Theology. Christianity Today,* vol. 27, no. 19 (December 16, 1983), pp. 55-56.

Review of W.A. Whitehouse, *Creation, Science, and Theology. Zygon,* vol. 18, no. 4 (December 1983), pp. 480-82.

Review of Adrio König, *Here Am I! Spirituality Today,* vol. 35, no. 4 (Winter, 1983), pp. 369-70.

"The Catholic Bishops on War and Peace." *Center Journal,* vol. 3, no. 1 (Winter, 1983), pp. 163-76.

"The Integrity of the Gospel." *Pastoral Renewal,* vol. 8, no. 7 (February 1984), pp. 94, 96. Part of this is an excerpt from *The Future of Evangelical Christianity.*

Review of Virginia Ramey Mollenkott, *The Divine Feminine. Eternity,* vol. 35, no. 2 (February 1984), pp. 43-45.

Review of Helmut Gollwitzer, *An Introduction to Protestant Theology. TSF Bulletin,* vol. 7, no. 3 (January-February 1984), pp. 32, 33.

"Living God or Ideological Construct." Comparative review of Rosemary Ruether, *Sexism and God-Talk* and Sallie McFague, *Metaphorical Theology. The Reformed Journal,* vol. 34, no. 6 (June 1984), pp. 29-31.

"Sanctity." *Pastoral Renewal,* vol. 9, no. 1 (July-August 1984), pp. 15-16.

"Concerns and Hopes For the United Church of Christ." *Living Faith,* vol. 5, nos. 1 and 2 (Spring-Summer, 1984), pp. 41-45, 60.

"Christ and Culture: Do They Connect?" *Christianity Today,* vol. 28, no. 10 (July 13, 1984), pp. 54-58.

"In Defense of Biblical Authority." A review of D.A. Carson and John D. Woodbridge, eds., *Scripture and Truth. The Reformed Journal,* vol. 34, no. 9 (September 1984), pp. 28-30.

"The Need for a Confessing Church Today." *The Reformed Journal,* vol. 34, no. 11 (November 1984), pp. 10-15.

Review of Wolfhart Pannenberg, *Christian Spirituality. Spirituality Today,* vol. 36, no. 4 (Winter, 1984), pp. 366-68.

"Cause for Rejoicing," *Pastoral Renewal,* vol. 9, no. 5 (December 1984), pp. 79, 80.

"Forecast '85: Theology." *Eternity,* vol. 36, no. 1 (Jan. 1985), p. 32.

Scripture Index

Name Index

Subject Index